JANUARY 1

LOVE

ANCHOR SCRIPTURE: 1 CORINTHIANS 13:1-3

"If I speak in the tongues of men or of angels, but do not have love, I am only a resounding gong or a clanging cymbal. If I have the gift of prophecy and can fathom all mysteries and all knowledge, and if I have a faith that can move mountains, but do not have love, I am nothing. If I give all I possess to the poor and give over my body to hardship that I may boast, but do not have love, I gain nothing."

L-O-V-E is the missing link in Leadership.
Live Our Values Everyday (LOVE)
-Ilka V. Chavez

PRACTICAL STEPS FOR APPLICATION:

1. Examine yourself and your leadership, based on the factors of love in today's devotional, is there any area you have not been exhibiting love in your leadership, or you have shown more love for your desires than the people God has given you to lead?

2. Write down each of the areas you are not meeting up in the journal space on the next page.

3. Look for a scripture that addresses each of these areas and pray for the help of God to exhibit His love in that area. For example, if you notice you get angry easily, meditate on Proverbs 19:11, James 1:19-20 and the grace will be released to you.

4. As you go about your daily activities, consciously look for situations that you could work on those areas love is lacking. For example, if you notice you are impatient, intentionally choose to be patient in situations that you are about to be impatient and try to understand the situation from the other person's perspective.

5. Find an avenue to show love to someone you have not shown love to in a while by giving them something, a compliment, or a gift.

Journal

JANUARY 2

Maintaining Momentum

ANCHOR SCRIPTURE: PHILIPPIANS 3:12-14 (NIV)

"Not that I have already obtained all this, or have already arrived at my goal, but I press on to take hold of that for which Christ Jesus took hold of me. Brothers and sisters, I do not consider myself yet to have taken hold of it. But one thing I do: Forgetting what is behind and straining toward what is ahead, I press on toward the goal to win the prize for which God has called me heavenward in Christ Jesus."

Belief in oneself is incredibly infectious. It generates momentum, the collective force of which far outweighs any kernel of self-doubt that may creep in.

-Aimee Mullins

PRACTICAL STEPS FOR APPLICATION:

1. Examine yourself and your leadership and highlight at least seven areas in which you are losing or have lost momentum

2. Reflect on each of these areas and find out the point at which you lost momentum and the reasons behind the loss of momentum.

3. Look for a scripture that activates your momentum in each of these areas and pray for fresh momentum to press forward. For example, if you have lost momentum regarding investing and bringing up your children in the way of the Lord, meditate on 1 Timothy 3:4.

4. As you go about your daily activities, watch out for situations that cause you to lose momentum and rather than give up, move ahead with full force to achieve that goal.

5. Make confessions of Faith: "In my (mention the area of life that you are losing or have lost momentum), I press on to take hold of that for which Christ Jesus took hold of me. One thing I do, forgetting what is behind and straining toward what is ahead, I press on toward the goal to win the prize for which God has called me heavenward in Christ Jesus."

Journal

JANUARY 3

What you say and do

ANCHOR SCRIPTURE: PROVERBS 16:3

"Commit to the Lord whatever you do, and he will establish your plans."

We must let go of the life we have planned, so as to accept the one that is waiting for us."
-Joseph Campbell

PRACTICAL STEPS FOR APPLICATION:

1. Before you can commit your ways to God, you need to commit yourself first. Identify the areas of your life that you trust in yourself and lean on your own understanding than in God

2. Pray to God to help you commit what you say and do in these areas to him sincerely

3. Next time you are planning on a line of action or new project, invite God to collaborate with you and help you make the right decisions that please Him

4. Before you do or say anything, make sure you ask yourself this question, "Will God have me do or say this?"

5. Document your progress in this journal and give yourself points as you yield your ways to God more and trust less in yourself

Journal

JANUARY 4

Seeking Purpose

ANCHOR SCRIPTURE: HEBREWS 13:21

" Equip you with everything good for doing his will, and may he work in us what is pleasing to him, through Jesus Christ, to whom be glory for ever and ever."

"The meaning of life is to find your gift.
The purpose of life is to give it away."
- *Pablo Picasso*

PRACTICAL STEPS FOR APPLICATION:

1. Like an eagle, look for a time of separation from man and focus on God. Take your time to retreat to a place no man will disturb you or where work and other important things of life won't come up to distract you.

2. Take this journal, a bible, and a pen with you so you God can minister His purpose(s) to you as you seek Him in prayer in your place of separation.

3. If you cannot get the chance to do this, as you go about your daily routine tell God to open your eyes to see the things that signify your purpose and write each one down in the journal as God reveals it to you by His Spirit

4. After you have gotten your purpose(s), go through each one and tell God to lead you and help you focus on the right one per time.

Journal

JANUARY 5

Greener grass syndrome

ANCHOR SCRIPTURE: PSALM 1:3

"That person is like a tree planted by streams of water, which yields its fruit in season and whose leaf does not wither-whatever they do prospers."

"The grass isn't always greener on the other side!"
- *Ricky Gervais*

PRACTICAL STEPS FOR APPLICATION:

1. First step to eliminate the greener grass syndrome is to decide to stop comparing yourself to others

2. Take a pen and paper, and looking at your own current situation, list the things that are not working in it

3. Find out what God is saying and judge your grass only based on what God is saying about it.

4. What makes someone else's grass greener is the way they take care of it. From today, ensure that you go out of your way to acquire the necessary knowledge and take disciplined steps to make your grass also green enough for others and yourself to admire

Journal

JANUARY 6

Obey, Love, and Serve

ANCHOR SCRIPTURE: DEUTERONOMY 11:13-15

"So if you faithfully obey the commands I am giving you today—to love the LORD your God and to serve him with all your heart and with all your soul, then I will send rain on your land in its season, both autumn and spring rains, so that you may gather in your grain, new wine and olive oil. I will provide grass in the fields for your cattle, and you will eat and be satisfied."

"The purpose of human life is to serve, and to show compassion and the will to help others."
-Albert Schweitzer

PRACTICAL STEPS FOR APPLICATION:

1. Check your priorities and ensure that it is in this order; Love God, Obey His leading daily, serve the people He has put you over to lead with the whole of your heart. We need constant check to make sure we have not missed or misplaced any of these priorities

2. Say aloud to yourself "I have the Spirit of God and therefore, I love people sincerely! I am happy to serve others and to obey God because it is my nature. So, I do this every day without failing because I am empowered to! Hallelujah!"

3. Make it a duty to pray for someone every day.

4. Right now, set aside a personal journal. In that journal, write down the list of two people per day of whom you will be a blessing to every day of this week.

5. Record their reactions to these gestures in your journal.

Journal

JANUARY 7

Justice

ANCHOR SCRIPTURE: ISAIAH 56:1

"This is what the Lord says: "Maintain justice and do what is right, for my salvation is close at hand and my righteousness will soon be revealed."

"I have always found that mercy bears richer fruits than strict justice"
- *Abraham Lincoln*

PRACTICAL STEPS FOR APPLICATION:

1. Think through on how you have managed situations with erring people. Consider whether you handled it properly.

2. Think of how you could have been a better and more exemplary leader through your actions

3. Write out what you would do differently next time in the journal space.

Journal

JANUARY 8

Power

ANCHOR SCRIPTURE: ACTS 19:20

"In this way the word of the Lord spread widely and grew in power"

"The past cannot be changed. The future is yet in your power."
- *Unknown*

PRACTICAL STEPS FOR APPLICATION:

1. Take time to read the first 10 chapters in the book of Acts and notice the wisdom that produced the multiplication of the Church

2. As you read, make note of the leadership styles that the applied in the church, especially in Acts 6

3. In the journal space, make a list of new techniques to apply in your organization to ensure growth

Journal

JANUARY 9

Created in his image

ANCHOR SCRIPTURE: GENESIS 1:27

"So, God created mankind in his own image, in the image of God he created them; male and female he created them."

"Life isn't about finding yourself. Life is about creating yourself."
- *George Bernard Shaw*

PRACTICAL STEPS FOR APPLICATION:

1. Talk to someone who you lead and ask him or her for creative ideas on how better you could lead your people.

2. Collect the responses and examine them.

3. Modify and implement or discard them and ask another person.

4. In the journal space, write every idea you got.

Journal

JANUARY 10

Made Free

ANCHOR SCRIPTURE: JOHN 8:31-32

"To the Jews who had believed him, Jesus said, "If you hold to my teaching, you are really my disciples. Then you will know the truth, and the truth will set you free."

"Knowing is not enough; we must apply.
Willing is not enough; we must do."
- *Johann Wolfgang von Goethe*

PRACTICAL STEPS FOR APPLICATION:

1. Today, spend time in prayer and sincerely ask the Lord to search your heart and expose to you every way you have believed a lie.

2. In the journal space, note the things you feel the Spirit of the Lord is directing your heart to and see a mentor discuss them

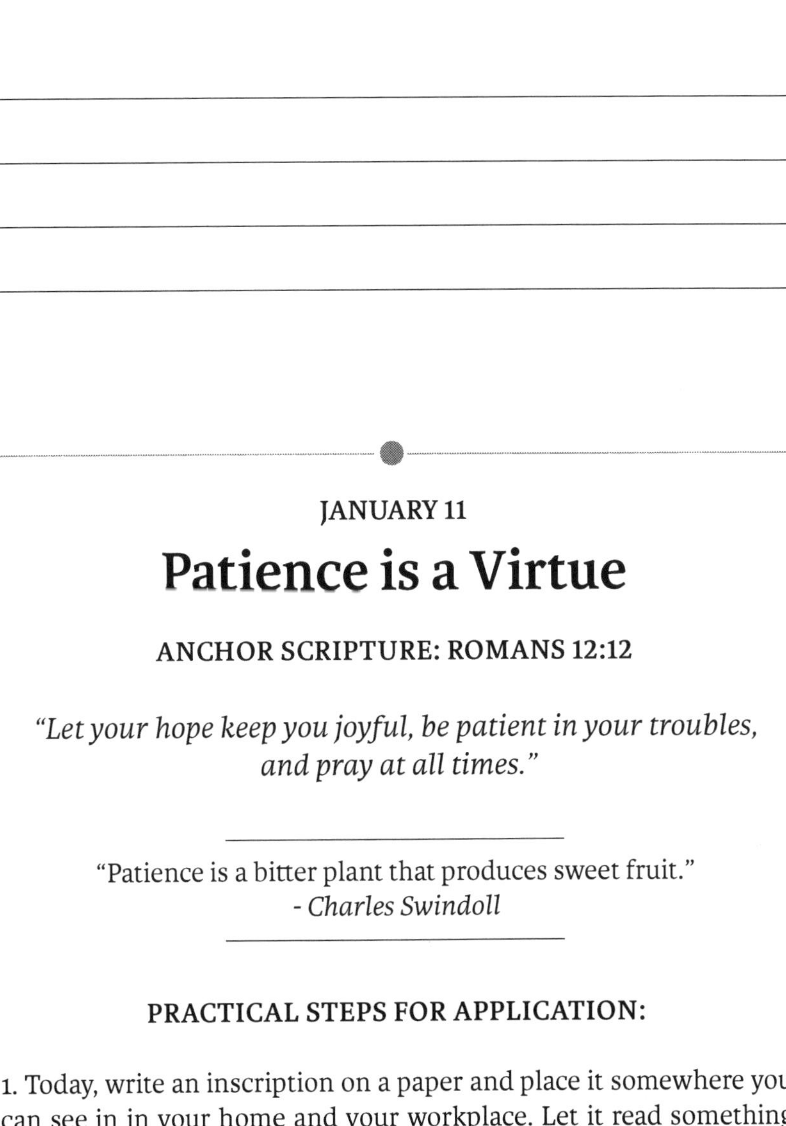

JANUARY 11

Patience is a Virtue

ANCHOR SCRIPTURE: ROMANS 12:12

"Let your hope keep you joyful, be patient in your troubles, and pray at all times."

"Patience is a bitter plant that produces sweet fruit."
- *Charles Swindoll*

PRACTICAL STEPS FOR APPLICATION:

1. Today, write an inscription on a paper and place it somewhere you can see in in your home and your workplace. Let it read something like "Patience is a Virtue" or "Patience is my Nature"

2. Make it a practice not to respond before or while someone is trying to speak and give the ample time after speaking before you respond.

3. Seek the counsel of a mentor or friend or spouse before responding to people on crucial matters today.

4. Note the actions and the results in the journal space

Journal

JANUARY 12

Seeking Happiness

ANCHOR SCRIPTURE: PSALM 37:4

"Take delight in the Lord, and he will give you the desires of your heart".

Your heart is where your treasure is, and you must find your treasure in order to make sense of everything."

- *Paulo Coelho*

PRACTICAL STEPS FOR APPLICATION:

1. Today you must appreciate yourself first. Remember every way you have served the lord and sacrificially obeyed his command. Make a note of five things you have sacrificed for your work sake and people you have helped through the years.

2. Thank God for enabling you with the grace to do this.

3. Decide to do more this month and year.

4. Set time aside every day or every week, to fill u the happiness bank in your heart by spending time with God and God alone at that hour.

JANUARY 13

Comfort

ANCHOR SCRIPTURE: 2 CORINTHIANS 1:3-4

"Praise be to God and Father of our Lord Jesus Christ, the Father of compassion and the God of all comfort, who comforts us in all our troubles, so that we can comfort those in any trouble with the comfort we ourselves receive from God."

"Cultivating compassion for ourselves and others can bring balance and harmony to our lives in a way we never dreamed of."
- *Thubten Chodron*

PRACTICAL STEPS FOR APPLICATION:

1. Examine yourself and evaluate how much you have shown compassion in recent times.

2. Make a list of five situations where you have been selfless and have put the interest of others first.

3. Make another list of five situations where you have not been placed the interest of others as you should.

4. Investigate what happened in the second instance and try to remedy all five.

5. Record your observations as you do no 4 in the journal space

Journal

JANUARY 14

Leading in Excellence

ANCHOR SCRIPTURE: EPHESIANS 6:4

"Fathers, do not exasperate your children; instead, bring them up in the training and instruction of the Lord."

"We are what we repeatedly do. Excellence, then,
is not an act, but a habit."
- *Aristotle*

PRACTICAL STEPS FOR APPLICATION:

1. As a father, you are a leader in your family, talk to your children to know what they think of how well you have been doing as a father.
2. If you are a wife or child help your husband or father become

a better father today by first appreciating him with a remarks like "Dear father, I want you to know that we appreciate all you do for us and we couldn't find another better than you."

3. As a father, take time read a book on effective parenting.

JANUARY 15

Reactive or Proactive Prayer

ANCHOR SCRIPTURE: 1 THESSALONIANS 5:17-18

"Pray without ceasing. In everything give thanks: for this is the will of God in Christ Jesus concerning you."

"Is prayer your steering wheel or your spare tire?"
- *Corrie ten Boom*

PRACTICAL STEPS FOR APPLICATION:

1. Today, devote at least one hour to prayer; it could be in the morning or evening

2. Make a list of ten people you want to pray for and find ten scriptures to use in prayer for them

Journal

JANUARY 16

Wisdom and Wealth

ANCHOR SCRIPTURE: PSALM 49:20

"People who have wealth but lack understanding are like the beast that perish."

"The real measure of your wealth is how much you'd be worth if you lost all your money."
- *Unknown*

PRACTICAL STEPS FOR APPLICATION:

1. Today, it's time to return to the foundation of why you became a leader. Go and review your mission and vision statements

2. Check your plans and see where you are now and check if you are still on course.

3. Make a list of the things that have changed in your life within the past five years and identity how they contribute to your goals.

4. Plan today, to remain on course and discard those things that add nothing to the aims and objective in your life as a leader.

Journal

JANUARY 17

Adhesive

ANCHOR SCRIPTURE: COLOSSIANS 1:17

"He is before all things, and in him all things hold together."

Man is born broken. He lives by mending. The grace of God is glue.
- *Eugene*

PRACTICAL STEPS FOR APPLICATION:

1. Read Colossians 1 and John 1.

2. Meditate on these scriptures and cross-reference them with Genesis 1.

3. Ask and allow God's Spirit to speak to you and you ruminate.

4. Write down what inspiration you got in the journal space

Journal

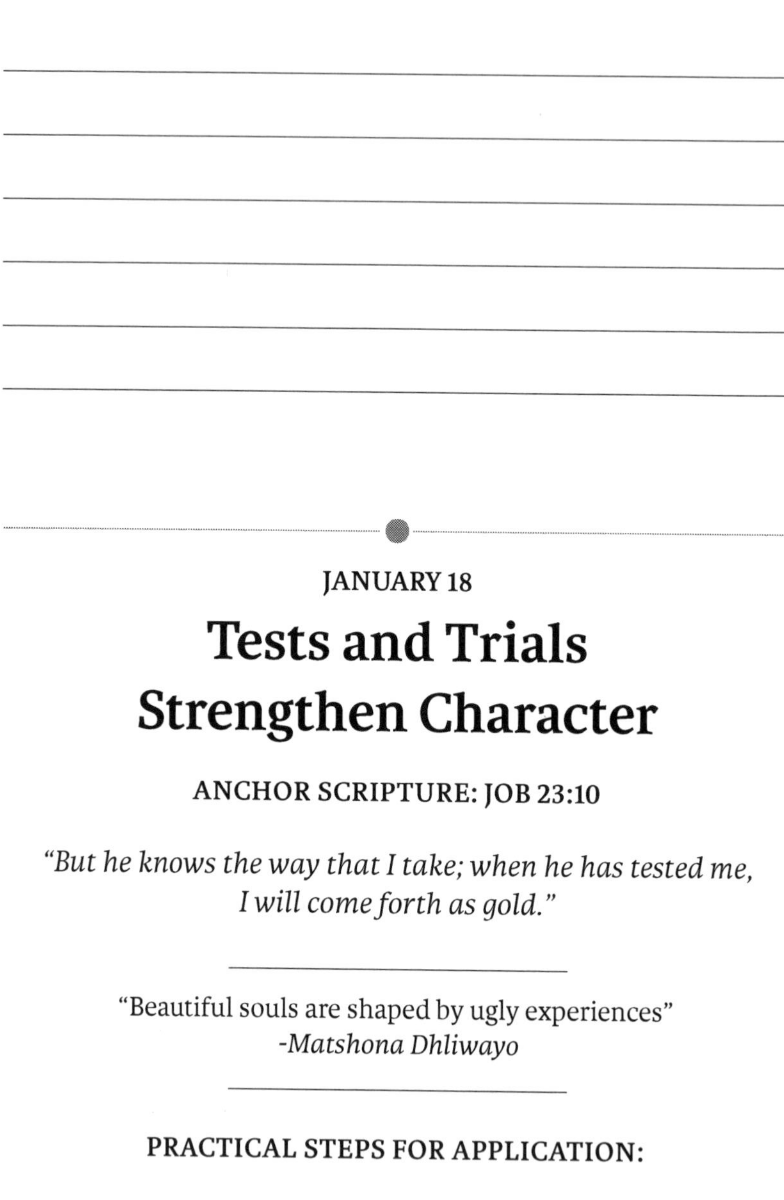

JANUARY 18

Tests and Trials Strengthen Character

ANCHOR SCRIPTURE: JOB 23:10

"But he knows the way that I take; when he has tested me, I will come forth as gold."

"Beautiful souls are shaped by ugly experiences"
-Matshona Dhliwayo

PRACTICAL STEPS FOR APPLICATION:

1. Track your progress today. Identify the trials you have had to go through and what character you think they should have formed in you.

2. Check to see if you have imbibed those values. Make it a duty to work on them and ask the Holy Spirit to help you.

Journal

JANUARY 19

Confidently Connected

ANCHOR SCRIPTURE: 1 JOHN 3:22

"And receive from him anything we ask, because we keep his commands and do what pleases him."

"It is not hard to obey when we love the one whom we obey."
- *Saint Ignatius*

PRACTICAL STEPS FOR APPLICATION:

1. Obeying God can only be done acceptably by the power of God through us, and this power comes from prayer and the word. Pray today, asking the Lord to strengthen your will to obey him

2. Read and meditate on the Romans 12.1-2 and John 15.1-12; 17.17

3. Evaluate how you have made your followers more obedient to God and teach them what has made and kept you obedient to God

Journal

JANUARY 20

Peace I Give You

ANCHOR SCRIPTURE: JOHN 14:27

"Peace I leave with you; my peace I give you. I do not give to you as the world gives. Do not let your hearts be troubled and do not be afraid."

"Peace is not something you wish for; it's something you make, something you do, something you are, and something you give away.

– *John Lennon*

PRACTICAL STEPS FOR APPLICATION:

1. Today, decide to live in the peace the Lord gives. This peace is based on the works of Jesus. Using the scriptures, meditate on the works of Jesus.

2. Read the real focus of the peace Jesus gives in Romans 5.1, John 16.32&33, Romans 14.17

3. Tell someone about the real peace focusing on Jesus brings

Journal

JANUARY 21

INFLUENCE

ANCHOR SCRIPTURE: GALATIANS 5:7-9

"You were running the race so well. Who has held you back from following the truth? It certainly isn't God, for he is the one who called you to freedom. This false teaching is like a little yeast that spreads through the whole batch of dough!"

"The key to successful leadership today is influence, not authority."
- Ken Blanchard

PRACTICAL STEPS FOR APPLICATION:

1. Reflect on Galatians 3 and 5

2. Write down the things that are influencing you and your leadership style today.

3. Check if they are taking you in the right or wrong direction with God's word.

4. Decide to readjust your life and leadership.

Journal

____

____

____

JANUARY 22

Wait and Grow

ANCHOR SCRIPTURE: PSALM 27:14

"Wait for the Lord; be strong and take heart and wait for the Lord."

When things do not go your way, remember that every challenge — every adversity — contains within it the seeds of opportunity and growth.
- Roy T. Bennett

PRACTICAL STEPS FOR APPLICATION:

1. Say this confession, "I have the grace of God upon my life because of his Spirit in me, therefore I am always ready and willing to wait and grow in God"

2. Say "I do not grumble and complain because I have longsuffering and temperance"

3. Talk to someone about your waiting experiences that have helped you grow over the years.

Journal

JANUARY 23

Rejoice Always

ANCHOR SCRIPTURE: 1 THESSALONIANS 5:16–18

"Rejoice always, pray continually, give thanks in all circumstances; for this is God's will for you in Christ Jesus."

"Rejoicing is grounded in gratitude, with a keen appreciation for yourself, others, your abundance, and the beauty around you."
- *Susan C. Young*

PRACTICAL STEPS FOR APPLICATION:

1. Make it a duty today to appreciate the very little things that people do for you today.

2. Thank God for the relationships in your life, the abilities you have, the place that you live and the people you lead

3. Thank God with an offering for the things he has done for you

Journal

JANUARY 24

Two Wrongs Don't Make a Right

ANCHOR SCRIPTURE: MATTHEW 5:39

"But I tell you, do not resist an evil person. If anyone slaps you on the right cheek, turn to them the other cheek also."

"If thy brother wrongs thee, remember not so much his wrong-doing, but more than that he is thy brother."
–*Epictetus*

PRACTICAL STEPS FOR APPLICATION:

1. Confess to yourself, "I am made in the image and likeness of God, I do not act unseemly towards others. I walk in love every day to everyone at every time!"

2. Send a note of apology to one person you may have offended in recent time.

3. Write the note down in the journal space

JANUARY 25

Managing Fear

ANCHOR SCRIPTURE: JAMES 4:7

"Submit yourselves, then, to God. Resist the devil, and he will flee from you."

"Don't let your fear of what could happen, make nothing happen."
- Doe Zantamata

PRACTICAL STEPS FOR APPLICATION:

1. Today, you need to practice submission, so plan a visit to your spiritual parent or mentor and serve them in any available capacity

2. Ask God to help you and the people you lead to be more submissive to him

3. Create a system to reward submission in your place of work

Journal

JANUARY 26

Victorious Living

ANCHOR SCRIPTURE: 1 CORINTHIANS 16:13-14

"Be on your guard; stand firm in the faith; be courageous; be strong. Do everything in love."

"Victorious living does not mean freedom from temptation, nor does it mean freedom from mistakes."
- *E. Stanley Jones*

PRACTICAL STEPS FOR APPLICATION:

1. Read 1 Corinthians 13 aloud and replace love or charity in the passage with your name

2. Set guards on your heart today, make a list of five things you would put at bay to maintain a victorious mind set

Journal

JANUARY 27

Contentment

ANCHOR SCRIPTURE: PHILIPPIANS 4:11

"Am not saying this because I am in need, for I have learned to be content whatever the circumstances."

"Many people lose the small joys in the hope for the big happiness."
- Pearl S. Buck

PRACTICAL STEPS FOR APPLICATION:

1. Today, decide to be contented with the things and people in your life.

2. Decide to teach your people on the essentials of Jesus' sermon on contentment

3. Make a list of excessive desires you hope to curb.

Journal

JANUARY 28

Forgotten Dreams

ANCHOR SCRIPTURE: EPHESIANS 3:20 (NLT)

"There is no fear in love. But perfect love drives out fear because fear has to do with punishment. The one who fears is not made perfect in love."

This morning do something different: When you wake up in the morning, wake your forgotten and forsaken dreams up as well, wake them up like an insisting rooster!

-Mehmet Murat Ildan

PRACTICAL STEPS FOR APPLICATION:

1. Write your forgotten dreams and longings.

2. Say yes to your dreams.

3. Start acting on them.

Journal

JANUARY 29

Stand United

ANCHOR SCRIPTURE: ECCLESIASTES 4:9-10

"Two are better than one, because they have a good return for their labor: if either of them falls down, one can help the other up. But pity anyone who falls and has no one to help them up."

"Two heads are better than one, not because either is infallible, but because they are unlikely to go wrong in the same direction."
- *C.S. Lewis*

PRACTICAL STEPS FOR APPLICATION:

1. Today, identify those things that are difficult and sapping your energy as a leader

2. Check to see if it could be that you need others to work with you, but you've been working on it alone

3. Identify potential partners and bring them on board.

Journal

JANUARY 30

Words and Works

ANCHOR SCRIPTURE: JAMES 2:18

"But someone will say, "You have faith; I have deeds." Show me your faith without deeds, and I will show you my faith by my deeds."

"Good works is giving to the poor and the helpless, but divine works is showing them their worth to the one who matters."
- *Criss Jami*

PRACTICAL STEPS FOR APPLICATION:

1. Pray and ask the Lord to forgive you for the times your profession of faith has not matched your actions of faith

2. Tell him to strengthen your heart for you to act aright always

Journal

JANUARY 31

Knowledge and Wisdom

ANCHOR SCRIPTURE: 1 KINGS 3:9

"So, give your servant a discerning heart to govern your people and to distinguish between right and wrong. For who is able to govern this great people of yours?"

"Knowledge without application is simply knowledge. Applying the knowledge to one's life is wisdom — and that is the ultimate virtue."
- *Kasi Kaye Iliopoulos*

PRACTICAL STEPS FOR APPLICATION:

1. Spend 30 minutes praying today asking the Lord to give you wisdom after reading James 1.5

2. Declare these words aloud "I walk in wisdom very day of my life"

3. Write out the areas you need wisdom today

Journal

February

FEBRUARY 1

God is Still Working

ANCHOR SCRIPTURE: HABAKKUK 1:5

"Look at the nations and watch and be utterly amazed. For I am going to do something in your days that you would not believe, even if you were told."

"You are where God wants you to be at this very moment. Every experience is part of His divine plan."

PRACTICAL STEPS FOR APPLICATION:

1. Make a list of three times you have cried to the Lord and he has heard your prayer and done something about your situation

2. Thank God for those times

3. Ask God to help you as you proceed in life

Journal

FEBRUARY 2

The Power of God's Grace

ANCHOR SCRIPTURE: PHILIPPIANS 2:13

"For it is God who works in you to will and to act in order to fulfill his good purpose."

"God answers the mess of life with one word: "grace."
- *Max Lucado*

PRACTICAL STEPS FOR APPLICATION:

1. Read and meditate on the story of Joseph in the Bible

2. Notice the places where God's grace helped him

3. Make thirty confessions of faith in God's grace you will write on a sheet of paper today

Journal

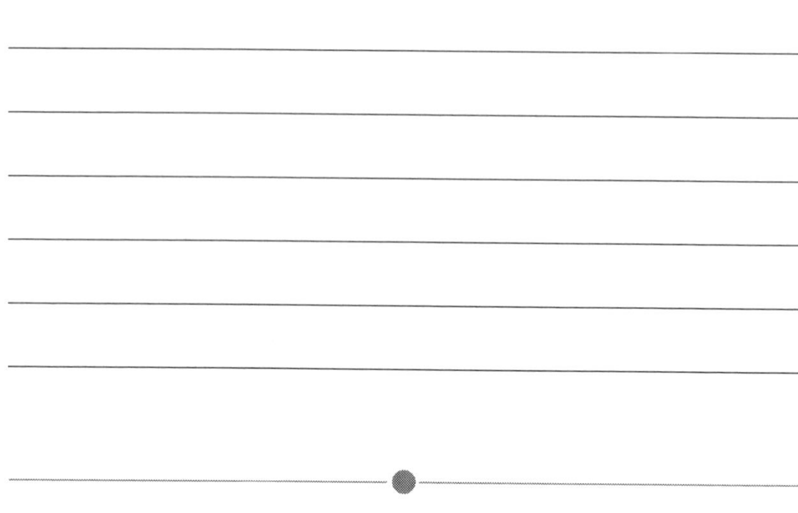

FEBRUARY 3

Equipped for Victory

ANCHOR SCRIPTURE: PSALM 119:98

"Your commands are always with me and make me wiser than my enemies."

"God has equipped you to handle difficult things. In fact, He has already planted the seeds of discipline and self-control inside you. You just have to water those seeds with His Word to make them grow!" - *Joyce Meyer*

PRACTICAL STEPS FOR APPLICATION:

1. Say aloud, "I am highly favored and graced by God. I am built for victory and success."

2. Confess "God loved me and chose me to make me victorious for his kingdom, therefore, I declare that victory is my heritage every day of my life till forever"

Journal

FEBRUARY 4

Self-Care

ANCHOR SCRIPTURE: MATTHEW 22:39

Jesus said, "You shall love your neighbor as yourself."

"Love yourself first and everything else falls into line.
You really have to love yourself to get anything done in this world."
- Lucille Ball

PRACTICAL STEPS FOR APPLICATION:

1. Write out three things you appreciate about yourself and recall how they began in your life.

2. Find out and write those things you would like to change about your life

3. Ask God to give you the wisdom to do these

Journal

FEBRUARY 5

Strength in numbers

ANCHOR SCRIPTURE: HEBREWS 10:24-25

"And let us consider how we may spur one another on toward love and good deeds, not giving up meeting together, as some are in the habit of doing, but encouraging one another—and all the more as you see the Day approaching..."

There is strength in numbers. Once we show the world that we're together, they can't stop us."
- *Cory Hardrict*

PRACTICAL STEPS FOR APPLICATION:

1. Make a note of three areas you may be experiencing challenges as a leader due to your inadequacy.

2. Think of people with more proficiency proven with results in those areas

3. Connect with them and seek for their help or a partnership

FEBRUARY 6

Favor

ANCHOR SCRIPTURE: PROVERBS 8.35

"For those who find me, find life and receive favor from the LORD."

Humility is the gateway into the grace and the favor of God."
- Harold Warner

PRACTICAL STEPS FOR APPLICATION:

1. Make it a duty to say as often as possible today, "I am blessed and highly favored today, I walk in the favor of God's Spirit every day."

2. Meditate on the goodness of God demonstrated by Christ and the power that lies in our words as believers

Journal

FEBRUARY 7

Are you ready to listen?

ANCHOR SCRIPTURE: PROVERBS 16:20

"Those who listen to instruction will prosper; those who trust the LORD will be joyful."

"One of the most sincere forms of respect is actually listening to what another has to say."
-Bryant H. McGill

PRACTICAL STEPS FOR APPLICATION:

1. In ten minutes, think of your life in the past with a view to seeing those things which the Lord, through his Spirit told you to do and you didn't

2. Consider where you would be now if you had obeyed

3. Decide to begin to walk in obedience from today

Journal

FEBRUARY 8

Greater is coming

ANCHOR SCRIPTURE: PSALM 139:16

"You saw me before I was born. Every day of my life was recorded in your book. Every moment was laid out before a single day had passed."

Do not give up when dark times come. The more storms you face in life, the stronger you'll be. Hold on. Your greater is coming.
- *Germany Kent*

PRACTICAL STEPS FOR APPLICATION:

1. Take time to consider how God has made the circumstances in your life to align together in bringing you where you are now

2. Thank God for those hard times you had from which you were molded to your current shape.

Journal

FEBRUARY 9

Let there be peace

ANCHOR SCRIPTURE: ROMANS 12:18

"If it is possible, as far as it depends on you, live at peace with everyone."

Peace is the result of retraining your mind to process life as it is, rather than as you think it should be."
- *Wayne Dyer*

PRACTICAL STEPS FOR APPLICATION:

1. As a leader, find someone who you may have offended and apologize today

2. Seek to make peace among parties in your tribe

Journal

FEBRUARY 10

Do Not Be Afraid

ANCHOR SCRIPTURE: LUKE 2:10

"But the angel said to them, "Do not be afraid. I bring you good news that will cause great joy for all the people."

"Why settle for a lesser vision? When you are destined for greatness!"
- *Laila Gifty Akita*

PRACTICAL STEPS FOR APPLICATION:

1. Today confront your fears, do the little things you fear most intentionally

2. Discuss your convictions about the believer's authority with a friend

3. Record the result of your discussion

FEBRUARY 11

Year-Round Joy

ANCHOR SCRIPTURE: PHILIPPIANS 1:27

"Whatever happens, conduct yourselves in a manner worthy of the gospel of Christ. Then, whether I come and see you or only hear about you in my absence, I will know that you stand firm in the one Spirit, striving together as one for the faith of the gospel."

"Year-round joy begins with gratitude for what you have."
- *Ilka V. Chavez*

PRACTICAL STEPS FOR APPLICATION:

1. Today find someone in your street with a need you can meet and meet that need

2. Send a thank you message to those in your life and appreciate them for being in your life.

Journal

FEBRUARY 12

The Sky is Not the Limit!

ANCHOR SCRIPTURE: PSALM 78:41-42

"Again, and again they put God to the test; they vexed the Holy One of Israel. They did not remember his power— the day he redeemed them from the oppressor..."

"The sky is not the limit. Your mind is."
- *Marilyn Monroe*

PRACTICAL STEPS FOR APPLICATION:

1. Faith comes by hearing. Go online and search out testimonies of Godin people's lives

2. Write out the major projects before you now and take them to God in prayer tell him to have the preeminence.

Journal

____

____

____

____

FEBRUARY 13

He Knows Your Order

ANCHOR SCRIPTURE: MATTHEW 6:8

"Do not be like them, for your Father knows what you need before you ask him."

"Let God's promises shine on your problems."
- Corrie ten Boom

PRACTICAL STEPS FOR APPLICATION:

1. Get a book and paper.

2. Head out to a secluded area to pray and after or during prayer begin

to listen to God for a word, vision, impression, or witness.

3. Write this down and achieve it

Journal

FEBRUARY 14

Purpose and Priorities

ANCHOR SCRIPTURE: EPHESIANS 1:11

"In him we have obtained an inheritance, having b een predestined according to the purpose of him who works all things according to the counsel of his will."

"Put First Things First"
- *Stephen Covey*

PRACTICAL STEPS FOR APPLICATION:

1. Write out 5 of your most tasking projects now and assign to them their purposes

2. From their purposes, arrange their priorities

Journal

FEBRUARY 15

Don't Fret the Old or the New Year

ANCHOR SCRIPTURE: PSALM 90:14

"Satisfy us in the morning with your unfailing love, that we may sing for joy and be glad all our days."

"Treat every day as a New Year"

PRACTICAL STEPS FOR APPLICATION:

1. Thank God for where you are today in destiny

2. Make list of all you wish to achieve in this phase of your life

3. Make concrete plans of how to get there

4. Submit the plans to a mentor

Journal

FEBRUARY 16

New Beginnings

ANCHOR SCRIPTURE: 2 CORINTHIANS 5:17

"Therefore, if anyone is in Christ, the new creation has come: The old has gone, the new is here!"

"Every page you have the courage to turn is a chance for a new beginning. Don't let fear keep you from turning the page"

PRACTICAL STEPS FOR APPLICATION:

1. Prayerfully make resolutions for your life today

2. Get a mentor to help monitor you as you follow through on your plans

Journal

FEBRUARY 17

Beauty

ANCHOR SCRIPTURE: 1 PETER 3:3-4

"Your beauty should not come from outward adornment, such as elaborate hairstyles and the wearing of gold jewelry or fine clothes. Rather, it should be that of your inner self, the unfading beauty of a gentle and quiet spirit, which is of great worth in God's sight."

"Everything has beauty, but not everyone sees it."
- *Confucius*

PRACTICAL STEPS FOR APPLICATION:

1. Buy a book on self-improvement and personal leadership

2. Cultivate people skills through good books and practice

3. Document your progress in this journal as you evolve

FEBRUARY 18

Courage

ANCHOR SCRIPTURE: 1 CORINTHIANS 16:13

"Be on your guard; stand firm in the faith; be courageous; be strong."

"Courage is resistance to fear, mastery of fear, not absence of fear."
- Mark Twain

PRACTICAL STEPS FOR APPLICATION:

1. Read 1 Corinthians 16 meditatively and apply the word to your life

2. See your mentor and discuss the challenges you face and the fears you have in your leadership role and life

Journal

FEBRUARY 19

Detachment

ANCHOR SCRIPTURE: LUKE 18:22

"When Jesus heard this, he said to him, "You still lack one thing. Sell everything you have and give to the poor, and you will have treasure in heaven. Then come, follow me."

"Your heart must become a sea of love. Your mind must become a river of detachment."
- *Sri Chinmoy*

PRACTICAL STEPS FOR APPLICATION:

1. Write out two things that have become idols in your heart

2. Abstain from these things by intentionally surrendering them to God. Decide to have no idols but God. List the steps you will take to detach from these two idols.

3. Pray that the Lord grant you grace and strength to detach from these idols.

Journal

FEBRUARY 20

Thanks for Your Gifts

ANCHOR SCRIPTURE: PHILIPPIANS 4:11-13

"I am not saying this because I am in need, for I have learned to be content whatever the circumstances."

"If what's ahead scares you and what's behind hurts you, then just look above. God never fails to help you. Trust Him."
– *Unknown*

PRACTICAL STEPS FOR APPLICATION:

1. Always give thanks over every new things God gives to you as a leader and over those you are leading. Begin a gratitude list.

2. Write a list of things that are causing you worry today and are preventing you from rejoicing then begin to give thanks to God over it.

Journal

FEBRUARY 21

Infinity

ANCHOR SCRIPTURE: EPHESIANS 3:20

"Now all glory to God, who is able, through his mighty power at work within us, to accomplish infinitely more than we might ask or think."

"Your greatest awakening comes, when you are aware about your infinite nature"
- Amit Ray

PRACTICAL STEPS FOR APPLICATION:

1. Write out five challenges you are presently passing through as a leader

2. Begin to prayer for the manifestation of God's power over it.

3. Confess daily your expectation over it.

Journal

FEBRUARY 22

Sin Makes Us Stupid

ANCHOR SCRIPTURE: HEBREWS 12:1

"Let us lay aside every weight, and the sin which so easily ensnares us."

The price of sin is very high, though now it may seem low; and if we let it go unchecked, its crippling power will grow."
—*Fitzhugh*

PRACTICAL STEPS FOR APPLICATION:

1. Write out five challenges you are presently passing through as a leader

2. Begin to prayer for the manifestation of God's power over it.

3. Confess daily your expectation over it.

Journal

FEBRUARY 23

Eliminating Distractions

ANCHOR SCRIPTURE: LUKE 8:7

"Other seed fell in the weeds; the weeds grew with it and strangled it."

"Starve your distractions, feed your focus."
– Unknown

PRACTICAL STEPS FOR APPLICATION:

1. Write out seven things that distract from focusing on spiritual things

2. Deliberately begin to ignore those things that distract you and put your focus on things that are needful.

Journal

FEBRUARY 24

Obey

ANCHOR SCRIPTURE: JOHN 14:15

"If you love me, you will obey what I command."

"When obedience ceases to be an irritant and becomes our quest, in that moment God will endow us with power."
- *Ezra Taft Benson*

PRACTICAL STEPS FOR APPLICATION:

1. Write out five instructions the Lord had given you that you've not obeyed

2. Deliberately step out to obey as a prove that you love God

3. Take a decision ever to always obey God's command.

Journal

FEBRUARY 25

Equality

ANCHOR SCRIPTURE: ROMANS 2:11

"For God does not show favoritism"

"We hold these truths to be self-evident:
that all men are created equal."
- *Martin Luther King Jr.*

PRACTICAL STEPS FOR APPLICATION:

1. Ask the Lord to forgive you in any way you have put yourself above your equals

2. Repent never to see yourself higher than others

3. Determine to begin to see people as equal as the bible state it.

Journal

FEBRUARY 26

Think Like a Winner

ANCHOR SCRIPTURE: 2 CORINTHIANS 4:8-9

"We are hard pressed on every side, but not crushed; perplexed, but not in despair; persecuted, but not abandoned; struck down, but not destroyed."

"If losing is mostly all you know, then it's obvious you haven't been thinking, acting, working, persisting, persevering, and walking like winners do."
- *Edmond Mbiaka*

PRACTICAL STEPS FOR APPLICATION:

1. Write out four challenges you are presently into

2. Declare God's word about it as a winner

3. Rejoice because you have victory already.

Journal

FEBRUARY 27

Have Your Cake and Eat It Too

ANCHOR SCRIPTURE: MATTHEW 6:24

"No one can serve two masters. Either you will hate the one and love the other, or you will be devoted to the one and despise the other. You cannot serve both God and money."

"You can't have it both ways. You can't have both free will and a benevolent higher power who protects you from yourself."
—*Arthur C. Clarke*

PRACTICAL STEPS FOR APPLICATION:

1. In sobriety, check in with yourself to identify some things contending with God in your life

2. Write it out in the journal

3. Pray earnestly for deliverance.

Journal

FEBRUARY 28

One Day at a Time

ANCHOR SCRIPTURE: PSALM 68:19

"Praise be to the Lord, to God our Savior, who daily bears our burdens."

Realize that the now is all we have. The past is just a story and the future is a complete mystery. This is it. Now.
- *Eckhart Tolle*

PRACTICAL STEPS FOR APPLICATION:

1 In your current life's journey, what are five burdens and five needs you are desperately facing? Write these in your journal today.

2. Pray and put it into God's care.

3. Do not panic about your need or burden. Trust God to supply your needs and relieve you of your burden.

Journal

MARCH 1

Vitality

ANCHOR SCRIPTURE: ISAIAH 40:31

"But those who hope in the Lord will renew their strength. They will soar on wings like eagles, they will run and not grow weary, they will walk and not be faint."

"Vitality shows in not only the ability to persist but the ability to start over."
- F. Scott Fitzgerald

PRACTICAL STEPS FOR APPLICATION:

1. Ask the Lord God to grant you grace and ability to wait on him.

2. Set a time today to wait on the Lord in prayer and fasting for renewal of strength.

Journal

MARCH 2

Provision

ANCHOR SCRIPTURE: PHILIPPIANS 4:19

"And my God will supply every need of yours according to his riches in glory in Christ Jesus."

"...You say to God, "I have never seen you provide for me."
God says to you, "You have never trusted Me."
- *Corallie Buchanan*

PRACTICAL STEPS FOR APPLICATION:

1. By faith, write out a list of your current needs and desires as a leader. List these below.

2. Pray and confess scriptures that relate to your need.

3. Believe that God has supplied your need to you already.

Journal

MARCH 3

Fear and Trust

ANCHOR SCRIPTURE: PSALM 56:3

"When I am afraid, I put my trust in you."

"Fear arises when we imagine that everything depends on us."
~ Elisabeth Elliot

PRACTICAL STEPS FOR APPLICATION:

1. List out five things that makes you afraid in leadership

2. Tell God in prayer how you have put your trust in him over the matter

Journal

MARCH 4

The Role Is Not the Reward

ANCHOR SCRIPTURE: JOHN 3:30

"He must become greater; I must become less."

"God cannot approve of a system of servitude, in which the master is guilty of assuming absolute power - of assuming God's place and relation towards his fellow-men."
- *Gerrit Smith*

PRACTICAL STEPS FOR APPLICATION:

1. Ask the Lord to subdue fleshy desires like ego and pride in your life

2. Ask the Lord God for humility to bring yourself into subjection to his will.

Journal

MARCH 5

Live Bold

ANCHOR SCRIPTURE: LUKE 12:32

"Do not be afraid, little flock, for your Father has been pleased to give you the kingdom."

Virtue is bold, and goodness never fearful.
William Shakespeare

PRACTICAL STEPS FOR APPLICATION:

1. Give thanks unto the Lord because you belong unto his kingdom

2. Pray a and ask the Lord to show you his intent over your life for his own kingdom

3. Determine to trust and obey him.

Journal

MARCH 6

Sticking to Your New Years' Resolution?

ANCHOR SCRIPTURE: LUKE 18:22 (NIV)

When Jesus heard this, he said to him, "You still lack one thing. Sell everything you have and give to the poor, and you will have treasure in heaven. Then come, follow me."

"Your heart must become a sea of love.
Your mind must become a river of detachment."
- *Sri Chinmoy*

PRACTICAL STEPS FOR APPLICATION:

1. Go back to your note where you wrote your resolution for the New Year. Highlight which resolutions you have kept and which you have had difficulty keeping and why. List those below and own your truth.

2 Decide to walk into the unfulfilled resolutions today. It is not too late.

3. Pray and ask the Lord's strengthen to enable you to carry out the resolutions successfully.

MARCH 7

Anchor Your Soul

ANCHOR SCRIPTURE: HEBREWS 6:19

"This hope we have as an anchor of the soul, a hope both sure and steadfast and one which enters within the veil..."

"We should not moor a ship with one anchor,
or our life with one hope."
- *Epictetus*

PRACTICAL STEPS FOR APPLICATION:

1. Decide to continue on your journey to be a steadfast leader. Remember hope is the anchor of your soul

2. Ask the Lord in prayer to give life to your hope that your soul may rejoice in it.

MARCH 8

Emotional Maturity

ANCHOR SCRIPTURE: 1 JOHN 4:7

"Dear friends, let us love one another, for love comes from God. Everyone who loves has been born of God and knows God."

"Fear is the glue that keeps you stuck.
Faith is the solvent that sets you free."
- *Shannon L. Alder*

PRACTICAL STEPS FOR APPLICATION:

1. Take a decision to show love to me people today as Christ did for you

2. Ask the Lord to help you grow spiritually and mature emotionally.

MARCH 9

Heart Trouble

ANCHOR SCRIPTURE: JOHN 14:1

*"Do not let your hearts be troubled.
You believe in God; believe also in me."*

"The heart of the human problem is the problem of the human heart."
- Adrian Rogers

PRACTICAL STEPS FOR APPLICATION:

1. Ask the Lord to cleanse you your heart and heal every wound in your heart

2. Forgive and release every offense and persons in your heart today

3. Ask the Lord God to guide your heart and comfort you in all time.

MARCH 10

Obey, Serve, and Love

ANCHOR SCRIPTURE: DEUTERONOMY 11:13-15

"So if you faithfully obey the commands I am giving you today—to love the LORD your God and to serve him with all your heart and with all your soul, then I will send rain on your land in its season, both autumn and spring rains, so that you may gather in your grain, new wine and olive oil. I will provide grass in the fields for your cattle, and you will eat and be satisfied."

"The purpose of human life is to serve, to show compassion and the will to help others."
- *Albert Schweitzer*

PRACTICAL STEPS FOR APPLICATION:

1. Find three commandments in scripture you are yet to obey and decide to obey them

2. Sing songs of love and praise to the Lord, saying you have chosen to love him forever

3. Ask God for grace to serve his will and please his heart.

MARCH 11

First Things First

ANCHOR SCRIPTURE: PSALM 119:2-3

"Blessed are those who keep his statutes and seek him with all their heart—they do no wrong but follow his ways."

"Most of us spend too much time on what is urgent and not enough time on what is important."
- *Stephen R. Covey*

PRACTICAL STEPS FOR APPLICATION:

1. Write out your priorities out and highlights those that pattern to the kingdom of God

2. Choose to carryout God's will first before any other thing.

Journal

MARCH 12

Pollution of Anger

ANCHOR SCRIPTURE: COLOSSIANS 3:8

"But now you must also rid yourselves of all such things as these: anger, rage, malice, slander, and filthy language from your lips."

"If you're going to pursue revenge, you'd better dig two graves"
- *Chinese proverb*

PRACTICAL STEPS FOR APPLICATION:

1. Highlight five things that makes you get angry and rage

2. Decide from now never to respond in anger to those things written down

3. Pray fervently for Grace to overcome the spirit of anger in your life.

Journal

MARCH 13

Idols in the Heart

ANCHOR SCRIPTURE: EZEKIEL 14:3

"Son of man, these leaders have set up idols in their hearts. They have embraced things that will make them fall into sin. Why should I listen to their requests?"

"Idolatry is really not good for anyone. Not even the idols."
- *John Bach*

PRACTICAL STEPS FOR APPLICATION:

1. Write out three things in your life that has replace your heart for God

2. Ask the Lord to forgive you over them

3. Repent never to allow them to take your heart for God

4. Pray for mercy.

Journal

MARCH 14

Temptation vs. Inspiration

ANCHOR SCRIPTURE: 1 CORINTHIANS 10:13

"No temptation has overtaken you except what is common to mankind. And God is faithful; he will not let you be tempted beyond what you can bear. But when you are tempted, he will also provide a way out so that you can endure it."

"Every time I say 'no' to a small temptation, I strengthen my will to say 'no' to a greater one."
- *Mother Angelica*

PRACTICAL STEPS FOR APPLICATION:

1. Read the Books of James chapter one and meditate over it

2. Ask the Lord to deliver you from all temptation that cannot be avoided

3. Seek the Lord for inspiration.

Journal

MARCH 15

Agape Love

ANCHOR SCRIPTURE: 1 JOHN 4:9

"This is how God showed his love among us: He sent his one and only Son into the world that we might live through him."

The only way love can last a lifetime is if it is unconditional. The truth is this: love is not determined by the one being loved but rather by the one choosing to love.
- *Stephen Kendrick*

PRACTICAL STEPS FOR APPLICATION:

1. Take a decision to tell and express agape love to ten people before the end of the day

2. Ask the Lord to shed the light of his love abroad your heart

3. Confess to love people as Christ loved you unconditionally always.

Journal

MARCH 16

Channeling Peace

ANCHOR SCRIPTURE: PHILIPPIANS 4:7

"And the peace of God, which transcends all understanding, will guard your hearts and your minds in Christ Jesus."

"Peace is the result of retraining your mind to process life as it is, rather than as you think it should be.

PRACTICAL STEPS FOR APPLICATION:

1. Make sure you go to settle all you conflict with people for peace sake

2. Pray to the Lord that you want to experience the fullness of God's peace in your life and family.

Journal

MARCH 17

All is Well... Be Cautious

ANCHOR SCRIPTURE: 1 PETER 5:8

"Be alert and of sober mind. Your enemy the devil prowls around like a roaring lion looking for someone to devour."

"Scars fade with time. And the ones that never go away, well, they build character, maturity, caution."
- *Erin McCarthy*

PRACTICAL STEPS FOR APPLICATION:

1. Study the life of Daniel to learn to be alert and be sober

2. Decide to pray in the mid night

3. Read a chapter in the Book of proverbs

Journal

MARCH 18

No Greater Love

ANCHOR SCRIPTURE: JOHN 3:16

"For God so loved the world that he gave his one and only Son, that whoever believes in him shall not perish but have eternal life."

"A true friend knows your weaknesses but shows you your strengths; feels your fears but fortifies your faith; sees your anxieties but frees your spirit; recognizes your disabilities but emphasizes your possibilities."
-William Arthur Ward

PRACTICAL STEPS FOR APPLICATION:

1. Do something sacrificial for someone today to express the great love of Christ

2. Tell someone about the great love of Jesus Christ

3. Mediate on the death and Resurrection of our Lord Jesus Christ.

Journal

MARCH 19

Know Better, Do Better

ANCHOR SCRIPTURE: JAMES 4:17

"Remember, it is sin to know what you ought to do and then not do it."

Do the best you can until you know better.
Then when you know better, do better.
- *Maya Angelou*

PRACTICAL STEPS FOR APPLICATION:

1. Write out the thing you know better but you've not been committed to them

2. Take a decision to act on one of them toady

3. Confess to always be a doer of God's word all the time.

Journal

MARCH 20

Detachment

ANCHOR SCRIPTURE: PROVERBS 23:4

"Do not wear yourself out to get rich;
have the wisdom to show restraint."

"Rich people have small TVs and big libraries, and poor people have small libraries and big TVs."
- *Zig Ziglar*

PRACTICAL STEPS FOR APPLICATION:

1. Decided to give something substantial today with a humble heart

2. Buy a book on management of resources and read it

3. Ask the Lord to bless you financially today.

Journal

MARCH 21

Face the Pain

ANCHOR SCRIPTURE: PSALM 147:3

"He heals the brokenhearted and binds up their wounds."

Real pain offers only two possible responses:
we can deal with it...or we can refuse to deal with it.
- *Matt Keller*

PRACTICAL STEPS FOR APPLICATION:

1. Highlight four pains you are passing through in your life

2. Decided to live above your present feelings on pain

3. Pray for healing and divine intervention of God's power in your marriage and family.

Journal

MARCH 22

Servant Leadership

ANCHOR SCRIPTURE: MARK 10:45

"Reminds us, for even the Son of Man came not to be served but to serve, and to give his life as a ransom for many."

"I have found that among its other benefits,
giving liberates the soul of the giver.
– Dr. Maya Angelou"

PRACTICAL STEPS FOR APPLICATION:

1. Take a decision today be to serve even as a leader not to be served

2. Take a practical step to prove it today.

Journal

MARCH 23

No Sacrifice, No Success

ANCHOR SCRIPTURE: ROMANS: 5:8

"But God demonstrates his own Love for us in this: while we were still sinners, Christ died for us."

Great achievement is usually born of great sacrifice
and is never the result of selfishness.
- *Napoleon Hill*

PRACTICAL STEPS FOR APPLICATION:

1. Write out four things you are hoping to achieve this year as a leader

2. Determine to begin to labor for success

3. Pray and ask the Lord to give you the ability to sacrifice for his kingdom

Journal

MARCH 24

Unique

ANCHOR SCRIPTURE: PSALM 139:14

"I praise you, for I am fearfully and wonderfully made. Wonderful are your works; my soul knows it very well."

What sets you apart can sometimes feel like a burden and it's not. And a lot of the time, it's what makes you great."
- *Emma Stone*

PRACTICAL STEPS FOR APPLICATION:

1. Search out ten scripture that speaks about who you are in Christ

2. Write those scripture out on the journal

3. Spend it reciting those scriptures in meditation

4. Rejoice for who God made you to be.

Journal

MARCH 25

Live, Laugh, Love

ANCHOR SCRIPTURE: PSALM 126:2-3

"Our mouths were filled with laughter, our tongues with songs of joy. Then it was said among the nations, "The Lord has done great things for them." The Lord has done great things for us, and we are filled with joy."

"Our attitude toward life determines life's attitude towards us"
- *John N. Mitchell*

PRACTICAL STEPS FOR APPLICATION:

1. Spend time today praising God

2. Decide to always respond your enemies with laughter

3. Ask the Lord to bestow upon you the spirit of joy

Journal

MARCH 26

Planted from Greatness

ANCHOR SCRIPTURE: PSALM 1:3

"He shall be like a tree Planted by the rivers of water, That brings forth its fruit in its season, Whose leaf also shall not wither; And whatever he does shall prosper."

Don't judge each day by the harvest you reap but
by the seeds that you plant.
– *Robert Louis Stevenson*

PRACTICAL STEPS FOR APPLICATION:

1. Study and meditate on Psalm chapter one verse 3 and Joshua chapter one verse eight

2. Start confessing great things into your life according to God's word.

Journal

MARCH 27

Get Out Of Your Own Way

ANCHOR SCRIPTURE: 2 TIMOTHY 1:7

"For God has not given us a spirit of fear and timidity, but of power, love, and self-discipline."

"The secret of change is to focus all of your energy not on fighting the old, but on building the new."
- *Socrates*

PRACTICAL STEPS FOR APPLICATION:

1. Write out your cares and fears in the journal

2. Now encourage yourself that you can do all things through Christ that strengthens you

3. As a leader confess to register this in your heart that you refuse to fear but God has endowed you with his power.

Journal

MARCH 28

Right or Kind

ANCHOR SCRIPTURE: COLOSSIANS 3:12

"Therefore, as God's chosen people, holy and dearly loved, clothe yourselves with compassion, kindness, humility, gentleness and patience."

Courage. Kindness. Friendship. Character. These are the qualities that define us as human beings, and propel us, on occasion, to greatness."
- *R.J. Palacio*

PRACTICAL STEPS FOR APPLICATION:

1. Take a decision to show kindness to three less privileged people you know in your surroundings

Journal

MARCH 29

Growing up is Hard to Do

ANCHOR SCRIPTURE: ECCLESIASTES 3:2

"A time to give birth and a time to die; A time to plant a nd a time to uproot what is planted."

"Life can only be understood backwards; but it must be lived forward."
- Soren Kierkegaard

PRACTICAL STEPS FOR APPLICATION:

1. Pray and ask the Lord to help you grow spiritually as you grow physically

2. Ask the Lord to comfort you in every challenges you into as of growth

Journal

MARCH 30

Obedience

ANCHOR SCRIPTURE: PHILIPPIANS 4:6-7

"Don't worry about anything; instead, pray about everything. Tell God what you need and thank him for all he has done. Then you will experience God's peace, which exceeds anything we can understand. His peace will guard your hearts and minds as you live in Christ Jesus"

Obedience is an act of faith; disobedience is the result of unbelief
-Edwin Louis Cole

PRACTICAL STEPS FOR APPLICATION:

1. Write out five expectations you desire God to do in this year

2. Search the scripture for principles that govern your request

3. Then start obeying them from today.

Journal

MARCH 31

Patience is Understanding

ANCHOR SCRIPTURE: PROVERBS 14:29

"Whoever is patient has great understanding,
but one who is quick-tempered displays folly."
Patience is not the ability to wait, but the ability
to keep a good attitude

PRACTICAL STEPS FOR APPLICATION:

1. Search out the scripture that speaks about your present challenges as a leader

2. Prayer for understanding of times and seasons

3. Decide to be patient and ask the Lord for grace.

Journal

APRIL 1

Harmony

ANCHOR SCRIPTURE: ROMANS 12:16

"Live in harmony with one another. Do not be proud but be willing to associate with people of low position. Do not be conceited."

"Harmony makes small things grow;
lack of it makes great things decay."
-Sallust

PRACTICAL STEPS FOR APPLICATION:

1. For you to live in harmony, patience is required; therefore, ask the Lord to help you to be patient

2. Log on to the link above and listen to the song

APRIL 2

Keep things simple

ANCHOR SCRIPTURE: LUKE 9:3

He said, "Don't load yourselves up with equipment. Keep it simple; you are the equipment."

Simplicity is ultimately a matter of focus.
-Ann Voskamp

PRACTICAL STEPS FOR APPLICATION:

1. Take a consideration of your current way of doing things

2. Look for ways you are not being simple

3. Cut off the excessive

Journal

APRIL 3

Lesson Learned

ANCHOR SCRIPTURE: PROVERBS 22:6

"Direct your children onto the right path, and when they are older, they will not leave it."

"More is taught than caught"

PRACTICAL STEPS FOR APPLICATION:

1. Start taking note of your words and actions

2. As a leader people including our children study us and follow us, therefore decide to speak right words at the right time and act according to God's word.

APRIL 4

Life with hope

ANCHOR SCRIPTURE: PSALM 34:18

"The Lord is close to the brokenhearted and saves those who are crushed in spirit."

"He who does not hope to win has already lost."
- *Jose Joaquin Olmedo*

PRACTICAL STEPS FOR APPLICATION:

1. When there is life there is hope therefore decide today to be happy and encourage yourself to be stronger in the Lord

2. Spend time reading your bible and praying through God's word because your hope finds strength in his word.

Journal

APRIL 5

Innovation in Action

ANCHOR SCRIPTURE: JAMES 1:4

"Let perseverance finish its work so that you may be mature and complete, not lacking anything."

"Success is just a pile of failures you are standing on"
- Dave Ramsey

PRACTICAL STEPS FOR APPLICATION:

1. Write out three things you have kept doing but failing

2. Decide now to depend on the Lord to guide you through

3. Pray to God for courage and wisdom.

Journal

APRIL 6

Intentional

ANCHOR SCRIPTURE: PSALM 139:16

"Your eyes saw my unformed body; all the days ordained for me were written in your book before one of them came to be."

Commitment with accountability closes the gap
between intention and results.
-Sandra Gallagher

PRACTICAL STEPS FOR APPLICATION:

1. Decide to be intentional today by writing out your needful things that should be done

2. Type it on your task reminder on your phone.

3. Make sure your goal is achieved at the end of the day

Journal

APRIL 7

Soar on Wings Like Eagles

ANCHOR SCRIPTURE: ISAIAH 40:31

"But those who hope in the LORD will renew their strength. They will soar on wings like eagles; they will run and not grow weary; they will walk and not be faint."

"Your wings are not broken. You already know how to fly."

PRACTICAL STEPS FOR APPLICATION:

1. You need the strength of God in your everyday life and that why you must wait upon Him every day. Spend a tangible time with God today as you worship and pray unto him

2. Decide to make it constant and be consistent because in consistency lies the power of your devotion.

Journal

APRIL 8

What's Your Priority?

ANCHOR SCRIPTURE: MATTHEW 6:33

"But seek first his kingdom and his righteousness, and all these things will be given to you as well."

PRACTICAL STEPS FOR APPLICATION:

1. This is a new week therefore figure out your priorities

2. Be determined to be successful this week in all your priorities

3. Make sure the God first others second and yourself last.

Journal

APRIL 9

Take Charge of Your Thoughts

ANCHOR SCRIPTURE: EPHESIANS 4:23-24

"To be made new in the attitude of your minds; and to put on the new self, created to be like God in true righteousness and holiness."

Happiness doesn't depend on who you are or what you have; it depends solely on what you think

- Dale Carnegie

PRACTICAL STEPS FOR APPLICATION:

1. Jesus in the book of Matthew chapter 5 during his temptation, he overcame the devil's temptation by the word of God saying, "It is written". Therefore, list out four thought that tempt you often

2. Search the right scripture for the temptation and start confessing it.

3. Also spend more of your time meditating on God's word

Journal

____

____

____

____

____

APRIL 10

Unfinished

ANCHOR SCRIPTURE: COLOSSIANS 4:17

And say to Archippus, "Be sure to carry out the ministry the Lord gave you."

"Two things rob people of their peace of mind; work unfinished and work not yet begun."
– Anonymous

PRACTICAL STEPS FOR APPLICATION:

1. As a leader there are many things in our hand to do but the ones God lay in our hand is most important, therefore find a quiet place the day and think deeply on what you are doing in life and write them out

2. Therefore out of all you've written highlight the ones God put in your care

3. Those you highlight are your pursuit therefore determine to face them and finish it.

4. Make sure you do ask for the help of the Lord

APRIL 11

Freedom from Fear

ANCHOR SCRIPTURE: ISAIAH 41:10

"Reminds us, don't be afraid, for I am with you. Don't be discouraged, for I am your God. I will strengthen you and help you. I will hold you up with my victorious right hand."

"Fear is the glue that keeps you stuck.
Faith is the solvent that sets you free."
- *Shannon L. Alder*

PRACTICAL STEPS FOR APPLICATION:

1. Write down all your fears you have

2. Meditate on Psalm 23 verse by verse

Journal

APRIL 12

The Blame Waltz

ANCHOR SCRIPTURE: GALATIANS 6:5

"For we are each responsible for our own conduct."

"Blaming others for your mess ups reflects on you"

PRACTICAL STEPS FOR APPLICATION:

1. Today, you must take responsibility for your mistakes, write down areas you have shifted blames and say to yourself "In this area, I am to be blamed, so I take responsibility"

2. Begin to check for what you could have done otherwise in those situations

3. Pray that the Lord will help you remedy the problems or do better next time

Journal

APRIL 13

The Power of Prayer

ANCHOR SCRIPTURE: ROMANS 12:12

"Be joyful in hope, patient in affliction, faithful in prayer."

"Prayer does not change God, but it changes him who prays."
- *Soren Kierkegaard*

PRACTICAL STEPS FOR APPLICATION:

1. Today, as a leader, make a list of people for whom you will daily pray for that Christ will be formed in them

2. Read Galatians 4.19, Colossians 4.12, and Romans 1.

3. Call or text the people you are praying for and encourage them, telling them of your prayers for them

Journal

APRIL 14

The Power of Appreciation

ANCHOR SCRIPTURE: PSALMS 92:1

"It is a good thing to give thanks unto the LORD, and to sing praises unto thy name, O most High"

Gratitude is a spiritual force that empowers you to scale higher.
You can't change to higher level without it.
- *Bishop Dr. Julius Soyinka*

PRACTICAL STEPS FOR APPLICATION:

1. Today, in your prayers, be only busy with searching for reasons to be thankful for to God.

2. Appreciate your subordinate, colleagues, and superiors today

APRIL 15

The Gift of Grace

ANCHOR SCRIPTURE: EPHESIANS 2:8

"For it is by grace you have been saved, through faith-- and this is not from yourselves, it is the gift of God."

Life is measured in love and positive contributions and moments of grace.
- *Carly Fiorina*

PRACTICAL STEPS FOR APPLICATION:

1. Extend the Grace of God to others today by encouraging your team to preach the gospel of Jesus to unsaved people.

2. Examine the message you have been preaching and living. Does it display the gift of grace to other people independent of their performance?

3. Decide today to teach that God accepts all who receive His grace irrespective of their performance

Journal

____

____

____

____

APRIL 16

Your Focus

ANCHOR SCRIPTURE: PHILIPPIANS 4:8

"Finally, brothers and sisters, whatever is true, whatever is noble, whatever is right, whatever is pure, whatever is lovely, whatever is admirable--if anything is excellent or praiseworthy--think about such things."

I always want to stay focused on who I am,
even as I'm discovering who I am.
- *Alicia Keys*

PRACTICAL STEPS FOR APPLICATION:

1. Your focus determines how you spend your time, make an inventory of how you have spent your time in the last 7 days.

2. Write down what should be your focus to achieve your desired results within record time

3. Take time to complete the exercise and decide to cut down on wasted time and reinvest it in the areas of your chosen focus.

APRIL 17

Faith, Love, Grace, and Wisdom

ANCHOR SCRIPTURE: EPHESIANS 6:2

"Honor your father and mother", which is the first commandment with a promise "so that it may go well with you and that you may enjoy long life on the earth."

"Mothers are faith, love, grace and wisdom in action"

PRACTICAL STEPS FOR APPLICATION:

1. Giving gifts is a gesture of honor. Send a gift to your parents or guardians today. It could also be to your parents in the Lord.

2. Send a thank you "thank you" note with it. Appreciate them and assure them of your love and honor

Journal

APRIL 18

Redemption

ANCHOR SCRIPTURE: EPHESIANS 1:7

"In him we have redemption through his blood, the forgiveness of sins, in accordance with the riches of God's grace."

Redemption is not perfection. The redeemed must realize their imperfections.
- *John Piper*

PRACTICAL STEPS FOR APPLICATION:

1. Begin a study about redemption by the blood of Jesus through faith

2. Journal as you study

Journal

APRIL 19

Refocus and Rise

ANCHOR SCRIPTURE: COLOSSIANS 3:2-

"Set your minds on things that are above, not on things that are on earth"

"You must learn a new way of thinking before you can master a new way to be."
-Marianne Williamson

PRACTICAL STEPS FOR APPLICATION:

1. Read Daniel chapter 8 and let it inspire you

2. Ask the Lord to strengthen you heart in times of trials

Journal

APRIL 20

Give What You Get

ANCHOR SCRIPTURE: MATTHEW 5:7

"Blessed are the merciful, for they will be shown mercy."

"The finer things in life cannot be purchased.
They can only be discovered through generosity."
- *Jeff Goins*

PRACTICAL STEPS FOR APPLICATION:

1. Make it a duty to be conscious of walking in love today

2. Start by making these confessions "I am born of love and I have the DNA of love in me, I walk in love effortlessly and I express the love of God without struggle. Hallelujah!"

Journal

APRIL 21

The Sweet Embrace of Life

ANCHOR SCRIPTURE: ECCLESIASTES 3:1

"There is a time for everything, and a season for every activity under the heavens."

Focus on the endless possibilities life is embracing you with at this very moment. Say YES to the next version of yourself

~ *Roxana*

PRACTICAL STEPS FOR APPLICATION:

1. Read Ecclesiastics chapter 3

2. Identify the season you are in now in your marriage, family, career, ministry, and leadership.

3. Project into the next phase you are going into in these areas and make plans ahead

APRIL 22

The Gift of Laughter

ANCHOR SCRIPTURE: PSALM 126:2

"Our mouths were filled with laughter, our tongues with songs of joy. Then it was said among the nations, "The Lord has done great things for them."

That ability to laugh at myself takes me from being a victim to being a victor.
- Annie Keys

PRACTICAL STEPS FOR APPLICATION:

1. The Bible encourages us to rejoice always because it is something we can do consciously. Today begin to rejoice dance and shout as you make this confession that follow

2. Hallelujah, I am redeemed forever to be a chosen generation and a holy person. I am the apple of the eyes of God.

3. Praise God, I am never going to experience lack, unfruitfulness, dryness, stagnation or any such things because God has blessed me, and I rejoice in that.

4. I walk in power and strength; I am always in favor and ever-increasing productivity. Praise God!

Journal

APRIL 23

Resilience

ANCHOR SCRIPTURE: MATTHEW 7:24

"Therefore everyone who hears these words of mine and puts them into practice is like a wise man who built his house on the rock."

"The difference between the wise and the foolish is resilience."

PRACTICAL STEPS FOR APPLICATION:

1. Take about 10 minutes to consider how fit you are emotionally, in family, social and spiritual

2. Seek the Lord's face on these areas and ask him to tell you something about them.

3. Begin putting those things to practice

Journal

APRIL 24

The Abundant Life

ANCHOR SCRIPTURE: JOHN 10:10

*"The thief comes only to steal and kill and destroy;
I came that they may have life and have it abundantly."*

So much has been given to me; I have no time
to ponder over that, which has been denied.
- *Helen Keller*

PRACTICAL STEPS FOR APPLICATION:

1. Say aloud "The Lord has anointed me to be successful and fulfilled, therefore I live in abundance every day of my life"

2. Search out and read the promises of God for you in the Bible.

3. Begin acting the word, act and speak as the word has described you

Journal

APRIL 25

Judging

ANCHOR SCRIPTURE: JOHN 4:11-12

"Brothers and sisters do not slander one another. Anyone who speaks against a brother or sister or judges them speaks against the law and judges it. When you judge the law, you are not keeping it, but sitting in judgment on it. There is only one Lawgiver and Judge, the one who is able to save and destroy. But you—who are you to judge your neighbor?"

"You judge someone not when you assess their position, but when you dismiss them as a person"
- Pastor J.D. Greer

PRACTICAL STEPS FOR APPLICATION:

1. Today begin to see others around you as equally children of God who God has not condemned

2. Decide to a focus on only the best about other people and ignore the bad sides.

APRIL 26

Purity of Motives

ANCHOR SCRIPTURE: PSALM 139:23-24

"Search me, God, and know my heart; test me and know my anxious thoughts. See if there is any offensive way in me and lead me in the way everlasting."

Many of our deepest motives come, not from an adult logic of how things work in the world, but out of something that is frozen from childhood.
- *Kazuo Ishiguro*

PRACTICAL STEPS FOR APPLICATION:

1. Ask the Lord to expose to you the things he wants to change in your life.

2. Ask him to help you turn a new leaf and make amends to others

Journal

APRIL 27

Doing Good

ANCHOR SCRIPTURE: ROMANS 2:7

"To those who by perseverance in doing good seek for glory and honor and immortality, eternal life"

I alone cannot change the world, but I can cast a stone across the water to create many ripples
- Mother Theresa

PRACTICAL STEPS FOR APPLICATION:

1. Today decide to act to others in the right way irrespective of their behavior or actions.

2. Make it a duty to say thank you and please. Say sorry even when you are right. Leave like Christ.

Journal

APRIL 28

A New Thing

ANCHOR SCRIPTURE: ISAIAH 43:18-19

"Forget the former things; do not dwell on the past. See, I am doing a new thing! Now it springs up; do you not perceive it? I am making a way in the wilderness and streams in the wasteland."

A new day: Be open enough to see opporunities. Be wise enough to be grateful. Be courageous enough to be happy.
- *Steve*

PRACTICAL STEPS FOR APPLICATION:

1. Today, you must talk to the Lord. Spend quality time in prayers and supplications. Ask God about his opinions and plans for the new times He is bringing you into

2. Write down your experience

Journal

APRIL 29

Your Best Version!

ANCHOR SCRIPTURE: 2 TIMOTHY 2:15

"Do your best to present yourself to God as one approved, a worker who has no need to be ashamed, rightly handling the word of truth."

Excellence is when who you are equals the best of who you can be.
- *Peng Joon*

PRACTICAL STEPS FOR APPLICATION:

1. Write out at least 10 things that you can do to become a better you.

2. Create an action plan to get started on them and get started. (You may talk to a personal development coach).

3. Affirm to yourself "When God thought of greatness, He created me, I am fearfully and wonderfully made".

Journal

APRIL 30

In the Midst of Tragedy

ANCHOR SCRIPTURE: JOHN 11:35

"Jesus wept."

"There is a saying in Tibetan, 'Tragedy should be utilized as a source of strength.' No matter what sort of difficulties, how painful experience is, if we lose our hope, that's our real disaster."
- *Dalai Lama*

PRACTICAL STEPS FOR APPLICATION:

1. Pray for missionaries that travel to the places where some of these tragedies occur.

2. Sow a seed into a ministry that ministers to the need of people affected by these incidents.

Journal

May

MAY 1

Honesty, the Best Policy

ANCHOR SCRIPTURE: COLOSSIANS 3:9

"Do not lie to each other, since you have taken off your old self with its practices."

PRACTICAL STEPS FOR APPLICATION:

1. Decide today to speak the truth no matter the consequences

2. Memorize Phil. 4:8

MAY 2

Loyalty

ANCHOR SCRIPTURE: PROVERBS 3:3

"Let love and faithfulness never leave you; bind them around your neck, write them on the tablet of your heart."

The foundation stones for a balanced success are honesty, character, integrity, faith, love, and loyalty.
-Zig Ziglar

PRACTICAL STEPS FOR APPLICATION:

1. Read 1 Sam 18-20

2. Write the lessons you learned and how you can apply them to your own relationships.

Journal

MAY 3

Maturation

ANCHOR SCRIPTURE: HOSEA 14:4

"I will heal their waywardness and love them freely, for my anger has turned away from them."

Some people see scars, and it is wounding they remember. To me they are proof of the fact that there is healing.
-Linda Hogan

PRACTICAL STEPS FOR APPLICATION:

1. Decide today to forgive everyone that has hurt you.

2. Offer to help someone grow through a painful situation.

Journal

MAY 4

Teamwork

ANCHOR SCRIPTURE: ECCLESIASTES 4:9-10

"Two are better than one because they have a good return for their labor: If either of them falls down; one can help the other up. But pity anyone who falls and has no one to help them up."

Talent wins games, but teamwork and intelligence
wins championships.
- *Michael Jordan*

PRACTICAL STEPS FOR APPLICATION:

1. Do something special for those that work with you.

2. Send an appreciatory note to your spouse, telling him/her how much he/she has been a blessing.

Journal

MAY 5

Traveling Mercies

ANCHOR SCRIPTURE: PSALM 71:6

"From birth I have relied on you; you brought me forth from my mother's womb."

Twenty years from now you will be more disappointed by the things that you didn't do than by the ones you did do, so throw off the bowlines, sail away from safe harbor, catch the trade winds in your sails. Explore, Dream, Discover.

- *Mark Twain*

PRACTICAL STEPS FOR APPLICATION:

1. Thank God for the gift of prayer and great friends.

2. Send a "Thank you" note to your friends who have contributed immensely to your life in the last decade.

3. Make a list of your friends and pray for them, mention their names.

Journal

____

____

____

____

____

MAY 6

Titles

ANCHOR SCRIPTURE: JONAH 2:8

"Those who pay regard to vain idols forsake their hope of steadfast love."

A boss loves power; a leader loves people.
- Amit Kalantri

PRACTICAL STEPS FOR APPLICATION:

1. Read and meditate on Phil. 2:5-11

2. Ask 10 of your close friends what they think about you.

Journal

MAY 7

Assumptions

ANCHOR SCRIPTURE: PROVERBS 18:13

"Spouting off before listening to the facts is both shameful and foolish."

Assumptions are the termites of relationships.
- Henry Winkler

PRACTICAL STEPS FOR APPLICATION:

1. Have you judged anyone wrongly? Walk up to them today and apologize. Let them know how sorry you are, and what you are willing to do to restore the relationship.

2. Have you been judged wrongly? Prayerfully walk up to the person who has judged you wrongly and try and make understand what the facts are and restore the relationship.

Journal

MAY 8

What you Focus on Grows

ANCHOR SCRIPTURE: PROVERBS 23:7

"For as he thinks in his heart, so is he..."

What you focus on grows, what you think about expands,
and what you dwell upon determines your destiny.
-Robin Sharma

PRACTICAL STEPS FOR APPLICATION:

1. Memorize Phil. 4:8

2. Make a list of your friends and hysteric those that put you down with discouraging words and actions and keep them at a distance.

3. Take a T.V break today.

Journal

MAY 9

Unplugged

ANCHOR SCRIPTURE: JOHN 15:5

"Yes, I am the vine; you are the branches. Those who remain in me, and I in them, will produce much fruit. For apart from me you can do nothing."

"Sometimes we need to disconnect in order to reconnect with what matters."

PRACTICAL STEPS FOR APPLICATION:

1. Make an inventory of 5 things that you can't do without in a week.

2. Of the 5 things outlined above, write out the 3 which add the most value to you and those around you.

3. Make up your mind to spend more time doing these 3 things.

Journal

MAY 10

Conflict in Compromise

ANCHOR SCRIPTURE: 2 TIMOTHY 2:4

"No soldier gets entangled in civilian pursuits, since his aim is to please the one who enlisted him."

Conflict cannot survive without your participation.
-Wayne Dyer

PRACTICAL STEPS FOR APPLICATION:

1. Whenever you're in a conflict, put yourself in the shoes of the other person.

2. Decide today to understand others before you get them to understand you.

Journal

MAY 11

Short Sighted

ANCHOR SCRIPTURE: 2 PETER 1:9

"For he who lacks these things is short sighted, even to blindness, and has forgotten that he was cleansed from his old sins."

"A short-sighted vision leads to missed blessings"

PRACTICAL STEPS FOR APPLICATION:

1. What would your life look like in 10 years? Take a pen and paper and write out your answers.

2. Outline what things you will have to give up attaining to this perfect picture.

3. Look out for people that are successful in these areas and become friends with them.

4. Share your vision with someone whom you trust, and will encourage you

5. Talk to somebody about what you learned today.

MAY 12

People Pleasing

ANCHOR SCRIPTURE: GALATIANS 1:10

"Am I now trying to win the approval of human beings, or of God? Or am I trying to please people? If I were still trying to please people, I would not be a servant of Christ."

The key to failure is trying to please everybody.
- Bill Cosby

PRACTICAL STEPS FOR APPLICATION:

1. Ask yourself this all-important question "Why do I do the things that I do?" Be sincere with yourself and document your answers.

2. Make up your mind to perform for the audience of one, Christ.

Journal

MAY 13

Pay It Forward

ANCHOR SCRIPTURE: GALATIANS 6:9

"Let us not become weary in doing good, for at the proper time we will reap a harvest if we do not give up."

"Our actions are like ships which we may watch set out to sea, and not know when or with what cargo they will return to port."
- *Iris Murdoch*

PRACTICAL STEPS FOR APPLICATION:

1. Appreciate the Lord for the opportunity to be a channel of blessing to others.

2. Decide today to consciously show kindness to everyone you come across.

3. Do something nice for someone who can't reciprocate your gesture.

Journal

MAY 14

Seek Wisdom

ANCHOR SCRIPTURE: PROVERBS 4:6

"Do not forsake wisdom, and she will protect you; love her, and she will watch over you."

Don't gain the world and lose your soul; wisdom is better than silver or gold.

- *Bob Marley*

PRACTICAL STEPS FOR APPLICATION:

1. God's word is His wisdom bank. Today, make up your mind to be a student of the word.

2. Make a list of things that are not working out the way you would want them to.

3. Search the Scriptures for practical solutions to these pressing issues of concern and apply them.

Journal

MAY 15

Condemnation

ANCHOR SCRIPTURE: ROMANS 8:1

"Therefore, there is now no condemnation for those who are in Christ Jesus."

Don't be in a hurry to condemn because he doesn't do what you do or think as you think or as fast. There was a time when you didn't know what you know today.

-Malcolm X

PRACTICAL STEPS FOR APPLICATION:

1. Most times, condemnation comes from past mistakes. Highlight mistakes that you have made and the consequences.

2. Ask the Lord to help you change the things that you can change, to get over those that cannot be changed and move on.

3. Decide today to see the best in people.

MAY 16

The Vicious Cycle of Greener

ANCHOR SCRIPTURE: PHILIPPIANS 4:11-13

"I am not saying this because I am in need, for I have learned to be content whatever the circumstances. I know what it is to be in need, and I know what it is to have plenty. I have learned the secret of being content in any and every situation, whether well fed or hungry, whether living in plenty or in want. I can do all this through him who gives me strength."

Get busy watering your own grass so as not to notice whether it's greener elsewhere.
- *Karon Waddell*

PRACTICAL STEPS FOR APPLICATION:

1. Make a comprehensive list of all the things that you are thankful for.

2. Take out 10 minutes to imagine what your life would be like if you did not have them in your life.

3. Take out yet another 10 minutes to give thanks for these things.

4. Affirm to yourself "I have all that I need to achieve whatever feat I desire"

Journal

MAY 17

In Living Color

ANCHOR SCRIPTURE: GENESIS 9:13-14

"I have placed my rainbow in the clouds. It is the sign of my covenant with you and with all the earth. When I send clouds over the earth, the rainbow will appear in the clouds."

"Life is full of beautiful colors. It is up to us to know how to enjoy each of them."

PRACTICAL STEPS FOR APPLICATION:

1. Appreciate God for His precious promises and His ability to make them good.

2. Look around your life and declare God's promises over situations that you are not satisfied with.

3. Brighten someone's day today by telling them of the wonderful gift of salvation.

Journal

MAY 18

Selective Hearing

ANCHOR SCRIPTURE: ISAIAH 50:4

"The Sovereign LORD has given me a well-instructed tongue, to know the word that sustains the weary. He wakens me morning by morning, wakens my ear to listen like one being instructed."

Hearing is listening to what is said.
Listening is hearing what isn't said."
- *Simon Sinek*

PRACTICAL STEPS FOR APPLICATION:

1. Memorize Heb. 4:12.

2. Determine today to direct your affairs according to the dictates of God's irrespective of what others think or say.

Journal

MAY 19

Live in Peace

ANCHOR SCRIPTURE: ROMANS 12:18-19

"Do all that you can to live in peace with everyone. Dear friends, never take revenge. Leave that to the righteous anger of God. For the Scriptures say, "I will take revenge; I will pay them back."

Peace begins with a smile.
-Mother Teresa

PRACTICAL STEPS FOR APPLICATION:

1. Practice forgiveness in advance. Make up your mind to forgive those that wrong you even if they are not sorry.

2. Do a thorough background check on yourself and highlight areas where you have not been walking in love and ask the Lord to help you.

3. Decide today to make at least consciously and conscientiously one person feel good every day.

Journal

___

___

___

MAY 20

Taking Your Blessings for Granted

ANCHOR SCRIPTURE: ECCLESIASTES 7:1

"A good name is better than fine perfume, and the day of death better than the day of birth."

Not what we say about our blessings, but how we use them, is the true measure of our thanksgiving.
- *W.T. Purkiser*

PRACTICAL STEPS FOR APPLICATION:

1. Pick up your pen and make a list of 10 people who have had tremendous impact on your life, positively, and appreciate them.

2. Make a habit of saying "Thank you" consciously, even for the littlest favors.

3. Take out time today to meditate.

MAY 21

Journey

ANCHOR SCRIPTURE: ROMANS 5:3-5

"Not only so, but we also glory in our sufferings, because we know that suffering produces perseverance; perseverance, character; and character, hope. And hope does not put us to shame, because God's love has been poured out into our hearts through the Holy Spirit, who has been given to us."

Difficult roads often lead to beautiful destinations.
The best is yet to come.
- *Zig Ziglar*

PRACTICAL STEPS FOR APPLICATION:

1. Take time out today to celebrate yourself for hanging in this long, you deserve it.

2. With step 1 done, renew your commitment (Put it in writing) to following your dreams until they become realities

3. Affirm to yourself "My best is yet to come"

MAY 22

Excuses, Excuses, Excuses

ANCHOR SCRIPTURE: PROVERBS 6:4

"Don't put it off; do it now! Don't rest until you do."

Your breakthrough begins where your excuses end.
- Pastor Steven Furtick

PRACTICAL STEPS FOR APPLICATION:

1. Excuses may come in form of hurts, disappointments or even betrayal from a loved one. Decide today to first, forgive yourself of past errors, and others who may have caused you pain in the past.

2. Many a time, our excuses border around what we think we lack. Today, affirm to yourself "the Lord is my Shepherd, I have all that I need" Psalm 23:1

3. Make up your mind to never shift blames. Take responsibility for your actions.

Journal

MAY 23

Work in Progress (WIP)

ANCHOR SCRIPTURE: PHILIPPIANS 1:6

"Being confident of this, that he who began a good work in you will carry it on to completion until the day of Christ Jesus."

Every strike brings me closer to the next home run
- *Babe Ruth*

PRACTICAL STEPS FOR APPLICATION:

1. Make an inventory of projects that you are working on currently.

2. In front of each project write out why you decided to embark on it. Heb. 12:1-2

3. Break down each project in small, easily achievable goals.

4. Reward yourself after the successful completion of each goal.

Journal

MAY 24

Balance

ANCHOR SCRIPTURE: EPHESIANS 5:15

"Look carefully then how you walk, not as unwise but as wise."

Life is about balance. Be kind, but don't let people abuse you. Trust, but don't be deceived. Be content, but never stop improving yourself

- Zig Ziglar

PRACTICAL STEPS FOR APPLICATION:

1. Read Ecclesiastes chapter 3

2. Before you go to bed each night makes a list the 6 most important things you must do the next day. Let nothing interfere with the times that you set to accomplish these tasks.

3. Download a good e-planner that can help you organize your tasks and remind you of your tasks.

Journal

MAY 25

Secrets

ANCHOR SCRIPTURE: JOHN 8:32

"Then you will know the truth, and the truth will set you free."

Your visions will become clear only when you can look into your own heart. Who looks outside, dreams, who looks inside, awakes.
– *C.G. Jung*

PRACTICAL STEPS FOR APPLICATION:

1. Look around prayerfully for a trusted Christian mentor who you can share with, and receive godly counsel from

2. Reflect on each of these areas and find out the point at which you lost momentum and the reasons behind the loss of momentum.

3. Perhaps your secret is some wrong committed in the past or even an addiction, read Heb. 4:14-16, and affirm to yourself "There is no condemnation against me because I am in Christ Jesus"

Journal

MAY 26

Blessings and Lessons

ANCHOR SCRIPTURE: ROMANS 8:28

"And we know that in all things God works for the good of those who love him, who have been called according to his purpose."

"Count your blessings and grow from your lesson"

PRACTICAL STEPS FOR APPLICATION:

1. Make a list of all the blessings you are thankful for. Psalm 103:1

2. Determine today to think through before making major decisions.

3. As you go about your daily activities, confess "Father I thank you because I know that all things, including this situation, is working out for my good"

4. At the end of each day, make an inventory in your journal space, of the things you are thankful for.

Journal

MAY 27

Planting Seeds

ANCHOR SCRIPTURE: GALATIANS 6:9

"And let us not grow weary of doing good, for in due season we will reap, if we do not give up."

Don't judge each day by the harvest you reap
but by the seeds that you plant.
- *Robert Louis Stevenson*

PRACTICAL STEPS FOR APPLICATION:

1. Memorize John 12:24

2. Make a list of 10 people that you have not spoken to in a long time and put a call through to them.

3. Look out for a community project that you can be part of.

4. As led by the Spirit of God seek out investment opportunities and make investments for your kids.

MAY 28

Take Action!

ANCHOR SCRIPTURE: JOHN 13:17

"Now that you know these things, you will be blessed if you do them."

An inch of movement will bring you closer to your goals than a mile of intention.
– Steve Maraboli

PRACTICAL STEPS FOR APPLICATION:

1. Make up your mind today to pay the required sacrifice for the success that you desire.

2. Perhaps you don't know where to start from? The secret of great men is in their stories. Make a list of at least 5 leaders that cut across the fields that you desire to succeed in.

3. Commit yourself to reading about them daily

4. Start!

Journal

MAY 29

Character Counts

ANCHOR SCRIPTURE: LUKE 8:17

"For there is nothing hidden that will not be disclosed, and nothing concealed that will not be known or brought out into the open."

Character is like a tree and reputation like a shadow. The shadow is what we think of it; the tree is the real thing.

PRACTICAL STEPS FOR APPLICATION:

1. Examine yourself (Be true to yourself) and highlight areas where you have character defects.

2. Before each character defect, write out how much pain has been caused to you and those around you.

3. Outline the joys that you will derive from becoming a better person
4. Make up your mind today to work on each character defect.

5. Get the help of a trusted friend that you can be accountable to.

Journal

MAY 30

Enslaved by Habits

ANCHOR SCRIPTURE: 1 CORINTHIANS 6:12 ESV

"All things are lawful for me," but not all things are helpful. "All things are lawful for me," but I will not be enslaved by anything."

Chains of habit are too light to be felt until they are too heavy to be broken.
-Warren Buffett

PRACTICAL STEPS FOR APPLICATION:

1. Take an inventory of your habits and identify any of the 5 mentioned above that you are a slave to

2. Write down the negative effects of each habit on your personal growth and family.

3. Draw up a plan towards getting free from the enslavement of each habit one after the other. Don't try to overcome all at once, follow the 'fasting' plan for each habit and record your growth in the journal below

MAY 31

Vulnerable

2 CORINTHIANS 12:9-10 (ESV)

But he said to me, "My grace is sufficient for you, for my power is made perfect in weakness." Therefore, I will boast all the more gladly of my weaknesses, so that the power of Christ may rest upon me. For the sake of Christ, then, I am content with weaknesses, insults, hardships, persecutions, and calamities. For when I am weak, then I am strong.

"Staying vulnerable is a risk we have to take if we want to experience connection."
– Brené Brown

PRACTICAL STEPS FOR APPLICATION:

1. In life there will surely be ups and down which we cannot escape. No man on this planet earth is perfectly strong because everyone is weak in one or more area of his life. Therefore, this is to make us humble and to seek for God's grace and depend on him to strength.

2. Pray according to Romans chapter eight verse twenty-six

3. Share your hidden vulnerabilities and weakness with your spouse or a trusted brother or friend.

JUNE 1

Breaking Chains

ANCHOR SCRIPTURE: 1 CORINTHIANS 10:13 (ESV)

"That no temptation has overtaken you that is not common to man. God is faithful, and he will not let you be tempted beyond your ability, but with the temptation he will also provide the way of escape, that you may be able to endure it."

"Chains of habit are too light to be felt until they're too heavy to be broken.
- *Warren Buffet*

PRACTICAL STEPS FOR APPLICATION:

1. Study and read James chapter one and meditate with a meek and sober heart.

2. Seek God for mercy and Grace according to Hebrews chapter for verse sixteen.

3. Be on your knees and cry unto the Lord.

Journal

JUNE 2

Reset

ANCHOR SCRIPTURE: 2 CORINTHIANS 5:17

"Therefore, if anyone is in Christ, the new creation has come: The old has gone, the new is here!"

"Every sunset is an opportunity to reset.
- *Richie Norton*

PRACTICAL STEPS FOR APPLICATION:

1. Study and meditate on Romans chapter twelve and Psalm chapter one hundred and ninety (119)

2. Decide to be humble and to accept what the Bible teaches

3. Ask God to open your understanding to who you are in Christ.

Journal

JUNE 3

Labor On Purpose

ANCHOR SCRIPTURE: 1 CORINTHIANS 15:58

"Therefore, my dear brothers and sisters, stand firm. Let nothing move you. Always give yourselves fully to the work of the Lord, because you know that your labor in the Lord is not in vain."

"Work on purpose so your labor is not in vain."

PRACTICAL STEPS FOR APPLICATION:

1. At some time as a leader we experience downfall in our labors but from today decide to be strong because the glory ahead of you cannot be compared with your present tribulation in labor

2. There is no birthing of child when no pregnancy and training there you labor is your groaning never relent because you will birth something great.

3. Ask the Lord to help your heart to be patient.

JUNE 4

Training Ground

ANCHOR SCRIPTURE: 2 TIMOTHY 3:16-17 (ESV)

"All Scripture is breathed out by God and profitable for teaching, for reproof, for correction, and for training in righteousness, that the man of God may be competent, e quipped for every good work."

"I hated every minute of training, but I said, don't quit. Suffer now and live the rest of your life as a champion".
- *Muhammad Ali*

PRACTICAL STEPS FOR APPLICATION:

1. Study and meditate on Hebrews chapter twelve.

2. For every product there is a process therefore never jump the process because is your training ground that your outcome which is your product can be great among others.

Journal

JUNE 5

Unbelievable

ANCHOR SCRIPTURE: HABAKKUK 1:5

"Look at the nations and watch and be utterly amazed, for I am going to do something in your days that you would not believe, even if you were told."

"Always remember to never forget"

PRACTICAL STEPS FOR APPLICATION:

1. Just as what happened to Mary was unbelievable even to her, but our God is great. Trust God for his greatness in your life

2. For every miracle you see, there is work involved. Keep on working, your miracle is near!

Journal

JUNE 6

Love Where You Are!

ANCHOR SCRIPTURE: ISAIAH 14:27

"For the Lord Almighty has purposed, and who can thwart him? His hand is stretched out, and who can turn it back?

"Do what you can, with what you have, where you are.
-Theodore Roosevelt

PRACTICAL STEPS FOR APPLICATION:

1. Read and study Isaiah chapter fourteen.

2. You need to love who you are because even God loves you than you love yourself.

3. Start a study on the book of Romans to know the implications of the love of Christ through his sacrifice.

Journal

JUNE 7

Carousel of Life

ANCHOR SCRIPTURE: ISAIAH 43:19 (NIV)

"See, I am doing a new thing! Now it springs up; do you not perceive it? I am making a way in the wilderness and streams in the wasteland"

"The carousel of life may have its ups and downs,
but it's still a great ride
- Unknown

PRACTICAL STEPS FOR APPLICATION:

1. No matter what you pass through just know there is an end to it.

2. Spend time praying and fellowshipping with the Lord.

3. Encourage yourself.

Journal

JUNE 8

Change-Character-Courage

ANCHOR SCRIPTURE: TITUS 2:7-8 (NIV)

"In everything set them an example by doing what is good. In your teaching show integrity, seriousness and soundness of speech that cannot be condemned, so that those who oppose you may be ashamed because they have nothing bad to say about us."

"Change makes you find your calling, your legacy, and God's divine plan for your life. Don't run from it.
– *Iman*

PRACTICAL STEPS FOR APPLICATION:

1. Decide today to be courageous

2. Always know that you can do all things through Christ that strengthens you.

Journal

JUNE 9

Once step at a time

ANCHOR SCRIPTURE: JAMES 1:4

"Let perseverance finish its work so that you may be mature and complete, not lacking anything"

"Sometimes the smallest step in the right direction ends up being the biggest step in your life.
- *Steve Maraboli*

PRACTICAL STEPS FOR APPLICATION:

1. There many times we don't achieve as a leader because of too many things we do at a time and it affect our focus therefore write out in you journal ten things you can't afford not to do.

2. Now highlight three most important out of the ten and determine to face it with focus.

3. Decide today to be focus on essential things.

Journal

JUNE 10

Inventory Your Habits

ANCHOR SCRIPTURE: 2 PETER 2:19 (NIV)

"For a man is a slave to whatever has mastered him"

"People do not decide their futures, they decide their habits and their habits decide their futures.

- F.M. Alexander

PRACTICAL STEPS FOR APPLICATION:

1. Read and study 2 Peter chapter two and the book of James chapter one. What

2. Pray fervently that the Lord should break every ungodly habit that has mastered you

Journal

JUNE 11

Giving Up Is Not An Option

ANCHOR SCRIPTURE: 2 CHRONICLES 15:7 (NIV)

*"But as for you, be strong and do not give up,
for your work will be rewarded."*

"If you quit on the process, you are quitting on the result
- *Idowu Koyenikan*

PRACTICAL STEPS FOR APPLICATION:

1. Take your time today to read the story of Ruth

2. Decide to be courageous and never give up on your responsibility and goals.

Journal

JUNE 12

Be A Lighthouse

ANCHOR SCRIPTURE: MATTHEW 5:14 (NIV)

"You are the light of the world. A town built on a hill cannot be hidden."

"Lighthouses don't go running all over an island looking for boats to save; they just stand there shining.
-Anne Lamott

PRACTICAL STEPS FOR APPLICATION:

1. Light is for the sight which is perception and darkness which is ignorance therefore decide today to enlighten a fellow and bring them into light.

Journal

JUNE 13

Keep It Simple

ANCHOR SCRIPTURE: MATTHEW 6:25

"Therefore, I tell you, do not worry about your life, what you will eat or drink; or about your body, what you will wear. Is not life more important than food, and the body more important than clothes?"

"Simplicity is the ultimate sophistication.
- *Leonardo da Vinci*

PRACTICAL STEPS FOR APPLICATION:

1. For you to be simple with life you need to be contented they seek for contentment

2. Always give thanks to God in all areas of your life.

Journal

JUNE 14

Grace to the Humble

ANCHOR SCRIPTURE: PROVERBS 3:34 (GNT)

"He has no use for conceited people but shows favor to those who are humble. "

"Humility is measured by your willingness to allow others to see who you really are in your own weaknesses and in brokenness. Not what we would like for others to see."
-Bill Bright.

PRACTICAL STEPS FOR APPLICATION:

1. Humility begins from your thinking therefore feed you yourself with God's word by spending thirty minutes to read and meditate on Psalm fifty-one.

2. Ask God to endow you with the grace to be humble.

Journal

JUNE 15

Walk Your Talk

ANCHOR SCRIPTURE: 1 TIMOTHY 4:12

"Let no one despise you for your youth, but set the believers an example in speech, in conduct, in love, in faith, in purity."

"The world is changed by your example, not by your opinion.
-Paulo Coelho

PRACTICAL STEPS FOR APPLICATION:

1. As a leader avoid procrastination

2. Make sure you walk what you talk your followers.

3. Decide to be a doer of God's word.

Journal

JUNE 16

The Words You Speak

ANCHOR SCRIPTURE: PROVERBS 16:24 (ESV)

"Gracious words are like a honeycomb, sweetness to the soul and health to the body"

"The words you speak become the house you live in.
– *Hafiz*

PRACTICAL STEPS FOR APPLICATION:

1. Take a decision today never to say what you don't mean; rather, determine to mean what you say and say what you mean.

2. Also determine to always speak words of grace.

3. Find a broken heart today and use your words to restore a heart from bitterness.

Journal

JUNE 17

Making A Living Or A Life

ANCHOR SCRIPTURE: ROMANS 12:2-(ESV)

"Do not be conformed to this world, but be transformed by the renewal of your mind, that by testing you may discern what is the will of God, what is good and acceptable and perfect."

"True masters are those who have chosen to make a life rather than a living.
- *Neale Donald Walsch*

PRACTICAL STEPS FOR APPLICATION:

1. When you make a living you live life for yourself only but when you make life you impart others with your resources therefore as leader increase your passion to see life change for good by imparting the resources God has trusted you with.

JUNE 18

To Judge or To Love...

ANCHOR SCRIPTURE: GALATIANS 6:1 (NIV)

"Brothers and sisters, if someone is caught in a sin, you who live by the Spirit should restore that person gently. But watch yourselves, or you also may be tempted."

An individual has not started living until he can rise above the narrow confines of his individualistic concerns to the broader concerns of all humanity.

- *Martin Luther King, Jr.*

PRACTICAL STEPS FOR APPLICATION:

1. Read 1 Corinthians 13.

2. Decide to help someone by standing for and by him/her in her fallen nature so as to help them get back on track with God.

Journal

JUNE 19

Success

ANCHOR SCRIPTURE: 1 KINGS 2:3 (NLT)

"Observe the requirements of the Lord your God and follow all his ways. Keep the decrees, commands, regulations, and laws written in the Law of Moses so that you will be successful in all you do and wherever you go"

"Success isn't just about what you accomplish in your life;
It's about what you inspire others to do.
– *Unknown*

PRACTICAL STEPS FOR APPLICATION:

1. As a leader your success count on your followers therefore encourage them

2. Decided to be courageous and don't be dismayed.

Journal

JUNE 20

Courage

ANCHOR SCRIPTURE: 1 CORINTHIANS 16:13(NIV)

"Be on your guard; stand firm in the faith;
be courageous; be strong"

"Courage is resistance to fear, mastery of fear, not absence of fear."
- Mark Twain

PRACTICAL STEPS FOR APPLICATION:

1. To be courageous is to be strong therefore study God's word on who you are in him

2. Confess scriptures that speaks about your abilities in God

Journal

JUNE 21

Worry Wart

Anchor Scripture: Psalm 55:22

*"Cast your cares on the LORD and he will sustain you;
he will never let the righteous be shaken"*

"Worrying does not empty tomorrow of its troubles,
it empties today of its strength.
-Corrie Ten Boom

PRACTICAL STEPS FOR APPLICATION:

1. Write out in the journal below four problem take you really care about

2. Pray about it and put your cares in God by having faith that he hears you.

JUNE 22

The Circle of Life

ANCHOR SCRIPTURE: ECCLESIASTES 1:3-5 (GW)

"What do people gain from all their hard work under the sun? Generations come, and generations go but the earth lasts forever. The sun rises, and the sun sets and then it rushes back to the place where it will rise again"

"The more we love the more we lose. The more we lose the more we learn. The more we learn the more we love. It comes full circle. Life is the school; love is the lesson. We cannot lose."
-Kate McGahan

PRACTICAL STEPS FOR APPLICATION:

1. Take your time today to study Ecclesiastes chapter one

2. Decided to do good to everyone either good or bad because life is a cycle.

Journal

JUNE 23

Disciplined

ANCHOR SCRIPTURE: PROVERBS 3:11-12

"My son, do not despise the Lord's discipline or be weary of his reproof, for the Lord reproves him whom he loves, as a father the son in whom he delights."

"Discipline is the refining fire by which talent becomes ability."
-Roy L. Smith

PRACTICAL STEPS FOR APPLICATION:

1. As a leader self-discipline is a power therefore give yourself certain orders and determine to live by it

2. Discipline helps you to live by principles therefore write out good principles on success and decide to follow it.

Journal

JUNE 24

Perfectly Broken

ANCHOR SCRIPTURE: REVELATION 21:5 (NIV)

"He who was seated on the throne said, "I am making everything new!" Then he said, "Write this down, for these words are trustworthy and true"

"Where there is ruin, there is hope for a treasure."
- *Rumi*

PRACTICAL STEPS FOR APPLICATION:

1. Study the book of Hebrews chapter twelve.

2. God loves the broken therefore go to God in prayer to mold you into his will and pleasure.

Journal

JUNE 25

Live, Laugh, Love

ANCHOR SCRIPTURE: 1 PETER 3:10-11

"Is a reminder "If you want to enjoy life and see many happy days, keep your tongue from speaking evil and your lips from telling lies. Turn away from evil and do good. Search for peace, and work to maintain it"

PRACTICAL STEPS FOR APPLICATION:

1. Today pray with your family and sing songs together in your home
2. Today, go out for picnic with your loved ones
3. Decide to laugh and smile more today

Journal

JUNE 26

Tomorrow is Not Promised

ANCHOR SCRIPTURE: JOHN 5:24 (ESV)

"Truly, truly, I say to you, whoever hears my word and believes him who sent me has eternal life. He does not come into judgment, but has passed from death to life"

"The best preparation for tomorrow is doing your best today."
- *H. Jackson Brown*

PRACTICAL STEPS FOR APPLICATION:

1. Now, take a decision to be careful and live right with your relationship even as a leader

2. Go and settle any conflict you are involve in with anyone

3. Determine to always be peaceful.

Journal

JUNE 27

Thank You

ANCHOR SCRIPTURE: 2 CORINTHIANS 4:15 (NIV)

"All this is for your benefit, so that the grace that is reaching more and more people may cause thanksgiving to overflow to the glory of God"

"Gratitude should not be just a reaction to getting what you want, but an all-the-time gratitude, the kind where you notice the little things and where you constantly look for the good even in unpleasant situations."

-Marelisa Fabrega

PRACTICAL STEPS FOR APPLICATION:

1. Gratitude opens door for more blessings therefore let your frequent words today be Thank You.

2. God loves it when you give thanks therefore spend fifteen minutes saying "_Thank You Jesus".

3. List 25 things for which you are grateful. Note when you are repeating. Expand what you are noticing.

Journal

JUNE 28

Give Thanks Always

ANCHOR SCRIPTURE: PSALM 100:4 (NIV)

"Enter his gates with thanksgiving and his courts with praise; give thanks to him and praise his name"

"When we focus on our gratitude, the tide of disappointment goes out and the tide of love rushes in."
-Kristin Armstrong

PRACTICAL STEPS FOR APPLICATION:

1. You cannot receive from God except you learn to give him thanks. Spend thirty minutes today with your family and followers in thanksgiving. Share, share, share.

2. Write out the troubles you are currently facing in life. Journal below and give thanks to God over it.

3. Also remember to give thanks to God for the little things you have today.

Journal

JUNE 29

Keep Climbing

ANCHOR SCRIPTURE: 2 CHRONICLES 15:7 (NIV)

"But as for you, be strong and courageous, for your work will be rewarded."

"Every mountain top is within reach if you just keep climbing"
~ Barry Finlay

PRACTICAL STEPS FOR APPLICATION:

1. Although your day today confess that you are strong and stronger than your challenges

2. Write out you goals for the month and ask the Lord to help to achieve them

Journal

JUNE 30

Giving Generously

ANCHOR SCRIPTURE: PROVERBS 3:27 (NIV)

"Do not withhold good from those to whom it is due, when it is in your power to act"

"I have found that among its other benefits, giving liberates the soul of the giver."
Maya Angelou

PRACTICAL STEPS FOR APPLICATION:

1. Giving put smiles in the face of the receiver therefore give a gift today to make someone smile

2. Encourage your followers and family to give with a pure heart

3. Be an example of a giver to the people around you

Journal

JULY 1

Hope Anyways

ANCHOR SCRIPTURE: ROMANS 5:5

"And hope does not put us to shame, because God's love has been poured out into our hearts through the Holy Spirit, who has been given to us."

"Life is a rope that swings us through hope.
Always believe that today is better than yesterday, and tomorrow will be much better than today...
- *Shermin Samuel*

PRACTICAL STEPS FOR APPLICATION:

1. Rewrite your expectations for this year in this journal and pray to the Lord to help you with achieving them.

2. Decide to trust God in all your plans and your ways.

Journal

JULY 2

Try or Trust

ANCHOR SCRIPTURE: JEREMIAH 7:8 NIV

"But look, you are trusting in deceptive words that are worthless."

"Never be afraid to trust an unknown future to a known God.
- *Corrie ten Boom*

PRACTICAL STEPS FOR APPLICATION:

1. Read Jeremiah chapter seven and Psalms chapter nine

2. Guard your heart from today never to doubt God in his abilities

3. Decide to depend on God in all your endeavors today.

Journal

JULY 3

Transformation

ANCHOR SCRIPTURE: 2 CORINTHIANS 5:17

"Therefore, if anyone is in Christ, the new creation has come: The old has gone, the new is here!"

"What the caterpillar calls the end of the world, the master calls a butterfly."
- Richard Bach

PRACTICAL STEPS FOR APPLICATION:

1. Go back to your dairy and see the things you suppose to do but you've not because of difficulty.

2. Summon courage today to take step in to the impossible.

3. Confess today that you can do all things.

JULY 4

Be a Rainbow

ANCHOR SCRIPTURE: GENESIS 9:13

"I have set my rainbow in the clouds, and it will be the sign of the covenant between me and the earth."

"Try to be a rainbow in someone else's cloud."
- *Dr. Maya Angelou*

PRACTICAL STEPS FOR APPLICATION:

1. Decide today to give someone hope by been a blessing to the person

2. Admire you family members and your followers especially today.

3. Have fun with your loved ones today.

Journal

JULY 5

Eyes on the Prize

ANCHOR SCRIPTURE: PHILIPPIANS 3:13-14 (NIV)

"Brothers and sisters, I do not consider myself yet to have taken hold of it. But one thing I do: Forgetting what is behind and straining toward what is ahead, I press on toward the goal to win the prize for which God has called me heavenward in Christ Jesus"

"Your most important work is always ahead of you, never behind you."
- Stephen R. Covey

PRACTICAL STEPS FOR APPLICATION:

1. Ups and down are part of life, therefore, encourage yourself and be strong to face life as it comes.

2. Spend forty minutes today to pray and seek God for strength to live above challenges.

JULY 6

Against All Odds

ANCHOR SCRIPTURE: ROMANS 4:18 (TPT)

Against all odds, when it looked hopeless, Abraham believed the promise and expected God to fulfill it. He took God at his word, and as a result he became the father of many nations. God's declaration over him came to pass: "Your descendants will be so many that they will be impossible to count!"

"Never let the odds keep you from doing what you know in your heart you were meant to do."
- *H. Jackson Brown, Jr.*

PRACTICAL STEPS FOR APPLICATION:

1. Take a break from the current task or assignment that seems to be impossible

2. Go back to your journal and spend time reminiscing on the original time the vison was gotten. Forget your current challenges and only focus on the benefits and lives that will be touched by the success of your vision.

3. Take time out to talk to God and seek His wisdom in prayer and studying books concerning those obstacles.

Journal

JULY 7

Refocus

ANCHOR SCRIPTURE: ROMANS 8:5 ESV

"For those who live according to the flesh set their minds on the things of the flesh, but those who live according to the Spirit set their minds on the things of the Spirit."

Happy New Year, Happy New Month and Happy January!

"JANUARY, the first month of the year, A perfect time to start all over again, changing energies and deserting old moods, new beginnings, new attitudes"
- *Charmaine J Forde*

PRACTICAL STEPS FOR APPLICATION:

1. You might not have achieved your goals although the year but is never too late therefore decide you can do it again

2. Spend time with God in quite mood to hear from him fresh instructions for the year.

3. Decide to love God this year

4. Say positive things to yourself that will help you focus.

JULY 8

The Power of Choosing Joy

ANCHOR SCRIPTURE: JOHN 15:10-11 (NIV)

"If you keep my commands, you will remain in my love, just as I have kept my Father's commands and remain in his love. I have told you this so that my joy may be in you and that your joy may be complete"

The joy we feel has little to do with the circumstances of our lives and everything to do with the focus of our lives."
- *Russell M. Nelson*

PRACTICAL STEPS FOR APPLICATION:

1. Play some songs of joy to refresh your mind

2. Read John chapter fifteen

Journal

JULY 9

Healing

ANCHOR SCRIPTURE: ISAIAH 58:8

"Then your light shall break forth like the dawn, and your healing shall spring up quickly."

"You will begin to heal when you let go of past hurts. Forgive those who have wronged you and learn to forgive yourself for your mistakes."
Anonymous

PRACTICAL STEPS FOR APPLICATION:

1. Forgive whoever and whatever offense of people in your heart right now and let go of it

2. If you have any pain or sickness in your body lay your hands on it and say "by his stripes I was healed therefore I command you infirmity (name whatever it is) to leave now in Jesus name!

3. Read and study Isaiah fifty-eight today.

Journal

JULY 10

Piece of the Puzzle

ANCHOR SCRIPTURE: EPHESIANS 2:21 (NIV)

"In him the whole building is joined together and rises to become a holy temple in the Lord."

"Without you, the puzzle is incomplete"

PRACTICAL STEPS FOR APPLICATION:

1. Confess today saying I will never give up until my dream come true
2. Write out your dreams and visions
3. Pray and ask the Lord to hasten his word to cone to pass.

Journal

JULY 11

When Trouble Comes...

ANCHOR SCRIPTURE: JAMES 1:2-4

"Reminds us, "Dear brothers and sisters, when troubles of any kind come your way, consider it an opportunity for great joy. For you know that when your faith is tested, your endurance has a chance to grow...."

PRACTICAL STEPS FOR APPLICATION:

1. Read Psalm chapter ninety-one and one hundred and one (121)

2. Give thanks to God today in your present troubles

3. Sing songs of comfort to yourself

JULY 12

Resilience

ANCHOR SCRIPTURE: ISAIAH 41:10 ESV

"Fear not, for I am with you; be not dismayed, for I am your God; I will strengthen you, I will help you, I will uphold you with my righteousness right hand."

"The human capacity for burden is like bamboo-far more flexible than you'd ever believe at first glance.

-Jodi Picoult

PRACTICAL STEPS FOR APPLICATION:

1. Go to your diary now and recite your best scripture verses written there

2. Rewrite five things God had told you he will do

3. Reaffirm those things and use it to pray.

Journal

JULY 13

Perspective

ANCHOR SCRIPTURE: ISAIAH 41:10 ESV

"Fear not, for I am with you; be not dismayed, for I am your God; I will strengthen you, I will help you, I will uphold you with my righteousness right hand."

"Empathy begins with understanding life from another person's perspective. Nobody has an objective experience of reality. It's all through our own individual prisms."
-Sterling K. Brown

PRACTICAL STEPS FOR APPLICATION:

1. Decide today to spend time reading. Pick a book and commit to read to completion.

2. Pray and seek the Lord to give understanding to have a right perspective

JULY 14

Elevated Thinking

ANCHOR SCRIPTURE: COLOSSIANS 3:2 (NIV)

"Set your minds on things above, not on earthly things."

"Your mind shines brightest when you enlighten others; your heart, when you encourage others; your soul, when you elevate others; and your life, when you empower others.

– *Matshona Dhilwayo*

PRACTICAL STEPS FOR APPLICATION:

1. Read and study Romans chapter eight

2. Spend twenty minutes meditating on this word saying, "he that is spiritually minded is life and peace but he that is carnally minded is death".

JULY 15

Covenant

ANCHOR SCRIPTURE: DEUTERONOMY 7:13 (NIV)

"He will love you and bless you and increase your numbers. He will bless the fruit of your womb, the crops of your land—your grain, new wine and olive oil—the calves of your herds and the lambs of your flocks in the land he swore to your ancestors to give you."

"God doesn't want us to have rigid rituals with Him. In the new covenant, He is more interested in having a relationship with us."
- *Joseph Prince*

PRACTICAL STEPS FOR APPLICATION:

1. Read Deuteronomy chapter seven.

2. Spend a quiet time with the Lord and talk to him and listen for him to talk to you.

JULY 16

Refuge

ANCHOR SCRIPTURE: PSALM 46:1 (NIV)

"God is our refuge and strength, an ever-present help in trouble."

"Education is an ornament in prosperity and a refuge in adversity."
- *Aristotle*

PRACTICAL STEPS FOR APPLICATION:

1. Write out five challenges you are facing presently

2. Search the scripture that speaks about your challenges

3. Confess scripture and speak against fear, doubt, depression, and other negative things.

4. Decide to always pray.

Journal

JULY 17

Having Faith

ANCHOR SCRIPTURE: MATTHEW 17:20 (NIV)

He replied, "Because you have so little faith. Truly I tell you, if you have faith as small as a mustard seed, you can say to this mountain, 'Move from here to there,' and it will move. Nothing will be impossible for you."

"You can't control everything. Sometimes you just need to relax and have faith that things will work out. Let go a little and just let life happen."
- *Kody Keplinger*

PRACTICAL STEPS FOR APPLICATION:

1. Write out 10 verses of scripture that talk about faith and read them out aloud.

JULY 18

Fired Up

ANCHOR SCRIPTURE: 2 CHRONICLES 15:7 (NIV)

"But as for you, be strong and do not give up, for your work will be rewarded."

"The struggle you're in today is developing the strength you need for tomorrow. Don't give up."
- *Robert Tew*

PRACTICAL STEPS FOR APPLICATION:

1. Make a list of 5 most important projects you are working on currently.

2. Below each project write 5 things that would go right or wrong if you didn't finish up the project.

JULY 19

Who Gets the Victory?

ANCHOR SCRIPTURE: PROVERBS 21:31

"The horse is made ready for the day of battle, but victory rests with the Lord."

"You cannot expect victory and plan for defeat"
-Joel Osteen

PRACTICAL STEPS FOR APPLICATION:

1. Examine yourself and highlight areas of your life where you have anxieties.

2. Commit each challenge to Godin prayer and make up your mind to never worry about them again.

Journal

JULY 20

Path of Life

ANCHOR SCRIPTURE: 1 CORINTHIANS 16:1

"Watch, stand fast in the faith, be brave, be strong." - NKJV

"You will find the path of life when your inner compass is ready."
– Debasish Mridha

PRACTICAL STEPS FOR APPLICATION:

1. Write out major decisions that you must make.

2. Take out time to pray over each decision.

3. With step 2 done, take out time to listen for by meditating on His word.

Journal

JULY 21

Facing Trials with Joy

ANCHOR SCRIPTURE: JAMES 1:2-12

"Count it all joy, my brothers, when you meet trials of various kinds, for you know that the testing of your faith produces steadfastness"

"The severe pain and the great trials we go through teach us the real essence of great joy"
-Ernest Agyemang Yeboah

PRACTICAL STEPS FOR APPLICATION:

1. Thank God today for His ability to save from the deepest depths of despair.

2. Make up your mind today to cast all your cares upon the Lord and trust Him.

JULY 22

God's Grace

ANCHOR SCRIPTURE: EPHESIANS 4:7

"But to every one of us is given grace according to the measure of the gift of Christ."

"Grace is given to heal the spiritually sick,
not to decorate spiritual heroes."
- *Martin Luther*

PRACTICAL STEPS FOR APPLICATION:

1. Memorize Jeremiah 29:11

2. Make this confession of faith "The grace of God is sufficient for me, and His strength is made perfect in my weakness"

Journal

JULY 23

Making Plans

ANCHOR SCRIPTURE: JEREMIAH 29:11

"For I know the plans I have for you," declares the Lord, "plans to prosper you and not to harm you, plans to give you hope and a future.

"God's plans are always exceedingly better than your plans"
- *Ilka V. Chavez*

PRACTICAL STEPS FOR APPLICATION:

1. Write you plans for this week and ask the Lord to help you bring them true

2. Pray and seek God's face for his wonderful plan over your life

3. Make a commitment to the Lord to always obey him.

Journal

JULY 24

Lacking Nothing

ANCHOR SCRIPTURE: PSALM 23:1–3

"Reminds us that the shepherd meets the sheep's every need: food, water, rest, safety, and direction. When we as believers follow our Shepherd, we, too, know that we will have all we need. We will not lack the necessities of life, for He knows exactly what we need."

"Be content with what you have; rejoice in the way things are. When you realize there is nothing lacking, the whole world belongs to you."
- *Lao Tzu*

PRACTICAL STEPS FOR APPLICATION:

1. Read and meditate on Psalm chapter twenty-three and chapter one hundred and twenty-one (121).

2. What you think you are lacking write them out and confess you have them already.

JULY 25

Fearing God

ANCHOR SCRIPTURE: PROVERBS 9:10

"The fear of the LORD is the beginning of wisdom, and knowledge of the Holy One is understanding."

"Even strength must bow to wisdom sometimes."
- Rick Riordan

PRACTICAL STEPS FOR APPLICATION:

1. Fearing the Lord is the key to key to wisdom meanwhile God's wisdom is in his word therefore take your time today to study the whole book of Proverbs.

Journal

JULY 26

Be the Light!

ANCHOR SCRIPTURE: MATTHEW 5:16

"In the same way, let your light shine before others, that they may see your good deeds and glorify your Father in heaven."

"Learn to light a candle in the darkest moments of someone's life. Be the light that helps others see; it is what gives life its deepest significance."
- *Roy T. Bennett*

PRACTICAL STEPS FOR APPLICATION:

1. The essence of your light to men to see it but you must shine it therefore shine God's light today by helping someone and preaching the Gospel

2. Read and study the book of Isaiah chapter sixty.

JULY 27

Taking Time

ANCHOR SCRIPTURE: MATTHEW 11:28

"Come to me, all who labor and are heavy laden, and I will give you rest." -ESV

"It's not about 'having' time. It's about making time. If it matters, you will make time."
- *Unknown*

PRACTICAL STEPS FOR APPLICATION:

1. Decide today to take an amazing time with God and fellowship with Him

2. Read and study The Gospel of John chapter sixteen.

Journal

JULY 28

Peace

ANCHOR SCRIPTURE: PHILIPPIANS 4:6-7

"Do not be anxious about anything, but in everything by prayer and supplication with thanksgiving let your requests be made known to God. And the peace of God, which surpasses all understanding, will guard your hearts and your minds in Christ Jesus.

"Peace cannot be kept by force, it can only be achieved by understanding"
- *Albert Einstein*

PRACTICAL STEPS FOR APPLICATION:

1. Take time today to think and confess the words God had spoken to you earlier before now

2. Praise brings peace therefore take twenty minutes today to praise God for his goodness.

JULY 29

The Golden Rule

ANCHOR SCRIPTURE: LUKE 6:31

"Do to others as you would have them do to you."

""We have committed the Golden Rule to memory;
let us now commit it to life."
- *Edwin Markham*

PRACTICAL STEPS FOR APPLICATION:

1. Take your time to study Luke chapter six

2. Decide to start or continue to do good to everyone despite of their status

3. Determine today to begin to treat people the way you want to be treated.

Journal

JULY 30

Stay the Course

ANCHOR SCRIPTURE: ISAIAH 41:10 (NIV)

"So do not fear, for I am with you: do not be dismayed, for I am your God. I will strengthen you and help you; I will uphold you with my righteous right hand."

" Face fear in the face, keep moving and stay the course.
Stick to plan A."
- *Ilka V. Chavez*

PRACTICAL STEPS FOR APPLICATION:

1. Take time to study the story of Job and be challenged to live a faithful life to God

2. Write out four things that brings fear to your heart

3. Prayer and confess that you are above them all because he that is from above is above all.

Journal

JULY 31

A Good Gift

ANCHOR SCRIPTURE: JAMES 1:17

"Every good gift and every perfect gift is from above, coming down from the Father of lights with whom there is no variation or shadow due to change."

"Health is the greatest gift, contentment the greatest wealth, faithfulness the best relationship."
-Buddha

PRACTICAL STEPS FOR APPLICATION:

1. Take time today to sing songs of praise and give thanks to God for every good gift

2. Confess and claim every good gift of good you have not seen yet.

AUGUST 1

Ohana

ANCHOR SCRIPTURE: GENESIS 12:3

"In thee [Abraham] shall all families of the earth be blessed"

Call it a clan, call it a network, call it a tribe, call it a family: whatever you call it, whoever you are, you need one.
- *Jane Howard*

PRACTICAL STEPS FOR APPLICATION:

1. Take out time to have fun with your family. You could have your parents over.

AUGUST 2

Freedom

ANCHOR SCRIPTURE: GALATIANS 5:1,13

"So, Christ has truly set us free. Now make sure that you stay free, and don't get tied up again in slavery to the law ... For you have been called to live in freedom, my brothers, and sisters. But don't use your freedom to satisfy your sinful nature. Instead, use your freedom to serve one another in love."

"Freeing yourself was one thing, claiming ownership of that freed self was another."
- *Toni Morrison*

PRACTICAL STEPS FOR APPLICATION:

1. Highlight in your life areas where you have struggles (Addictions, unwholesome habits etc.) and make bold declarations of your freedom in Christ.

2. Make up your mind to never go back to them.

AUGUST 3

Global Positioning System (GPS)

ANCHOR SCRIPTURE: PSALM 16:1-2

"Keep me safe, my God, for in you I take refuge. I say to the LORD, "You are my Lord; apart from you have no good thing."

"Trust your internal and spiritual GPS"
- *Ilka V. Chavez*

PRACTICAL STEPS FOR APPLICATION:

1. Commit all your ways into the hand of the Lord

2. Ask the Lord to always guide you in his right path

3. Therefore determine to always seek good before you take steps in life

4. Promise to always obey God's voice.

Journal

AUGUST 4

Searching for Purpose

ANCHOR SCRIPTURE: 2 TIMOTHY 3:16-17 (NIV)

"All Scripture is God-breathed and is useful for teaching, rebuking, correcting and training in righteousness, so that the servant of God may be thoroughly equipped for every good work."

"If you can tune into your purpose and really align with it, setting goals so that your vision is an expression of that purpose, then life flows much more easily."
- *Jack Canfield*

PRACTICAL STEPS FOR APPLICATION:

1. Go on a retreat to discover yourself and your purpose

2. Look around you, reflecting on your strength, passions, and natural talents.

3. Seek the face of God in prayer

AUGUST 5

The Discipline of Solitude

ANCHOR SCRIPTURE: MARK 1:35 (NIV)

"Very early in the morning, while it was dark, Jesus got up, left the house, and went off to a solitary place, where he prayed.

"Loneliness is inner emptiness; solitude is inner fulfillment.
-Richard Foster

PRACTICAL STEPS FOR APPLICATION:

1. Commit to spending some time in solitude at least once a week. With no phone, communication but just you, God, books, and your purpose

Journal

AUGUST 6

Tomorrow

ANCHOR SCRIPTURE: PROVERBS 6:4

"Don't put it off; do it now! Don't rest until you do."

The present is the ever-moving shadow that divides yesterday from tomorrow. In that lies hope.
-Frank Lloyd Wright

PRACTICAL STEPS FOR APPLICATION:

1. Identify all the things you have procrastinated on start making plans or taking actions on the already made plans

2. Set step by step goals to take you towards carrying out an assignment and follow it diligently

3. Audit yourself at the end of the day to see where you procrastinated and how you can do better next time

Journal

AUGUST 7

God's Perfect Timing

ANCHOR SCRIPTURE: HABAKKUK 2:3

"For still the vision awaits its appointed time; it hastens to the end—it will not lie. If it seems slow, wait for it; it will surely come; it will not delay."

"The right thing at the wrong time is the wrong thing."
-Joshua Harris

PRACTICAL STEPS FOR APPLICATION:

1. Pray and seek God's face to help your soul to be patience

2. Speak to yourself that you will never move faster than God's than timing for your life.

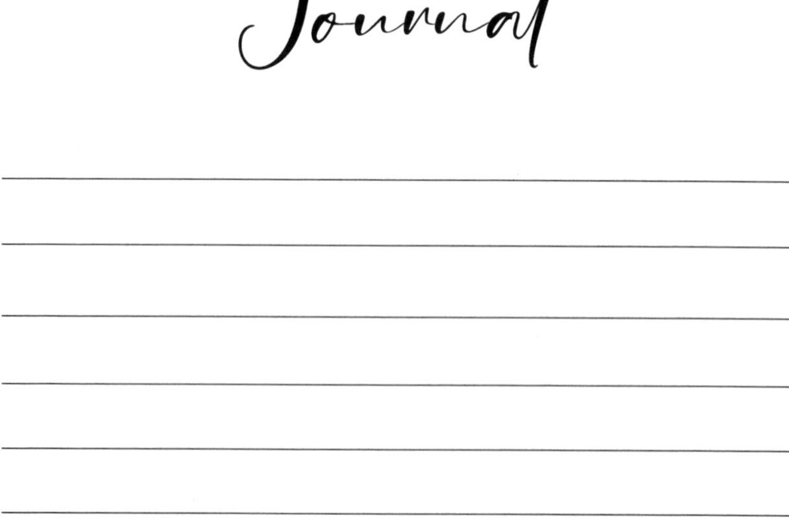

AUGUST 8

Living a Legacy

ANCHOR SCRIPTURE: PROVERBS 13:22

"A good man leaves an inheritance to his children's children."

"It's hard to say what I want my legacy to be when I'm long gone."
- Aaliyah

PRACTICAL STEPS FOR APPLICATION:

1. Today study the Bible and write out ten inheritance you have in God

2. Confess and call them forth to be manifested.

3. Share them with your children to build their own faith too

Journal

AUGUST 9

Living a Legacy

ANCHOR SCRIPTURE: 2 CHRONICLES 15:7

Be strong and do not give up, for your work will be rewarded."

"Keep your face to the sunshine and you cannot see a shadow."
- *Helen Keller*

PRACTICAL STEPS FOR APPLICATION:

1. As a leader ask yourself this question that "what kind of legacy am I laying down for people to follow"?

2. Ask the Lord to guide and teach you as to be a good leader.

Journal

AUGUST 10

No Greater Love

ANCHOR SCRIPTURE: JOHN 3:16

"For God so loved the world that he gave his one and only Son, that whoever believes in him shall not perish but have eternal life." (NIV)

"A true friend knows your weaknesses but shows you your strengths; feels your fears but fortifies your faith; sees your anxieties but frees your spirit; recognizes your disabilities but emphasizes your possibilities."

-William Arthur Ward

PRACTICAL STEPS FOR APPLICATION:

1. The best expression of love is giving therefore give out something today as God did by giving his only Son

2. Reach out to someone today and preach the Gospel of the great love of God them.

Journal

AUGUST 11

Dominion

ANCHOR SCRIPTURE: EPHESIANS 1:19-21

I also pray that you will understand the incredible greatness of God's power for us who believe him. This is the same mighty power that raised Christ from the dead and seated him in the place of honor at God's right hand in the heavenly realms. Now he is far above any ruler or authority or power or leader or anything else—not only in this world but also in the world to come.

"Living a natural life is living in dominion of a darkened mind"
-Sunday Adelaja

PRACTICAL STEPS FOR APPLICATION:

1. Study the book of Genesis chapter one with an understanding that Jesus had recovered our dominion back to us.

2. Rejoice and confess you have dominion.

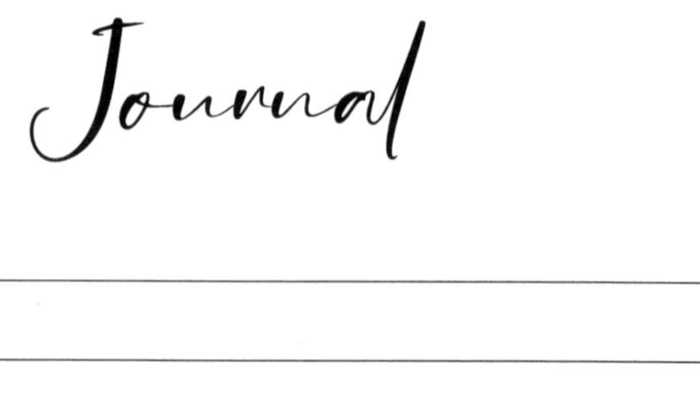

AUGUST 12

Let Go

ANCHOR SCRIPTURE: ISAIAH 43:18-19

"Do not remember the former things, Nor consider the things of old. Behold, I will do a new thing, Now it shall spring forth; Shall you not know it? I will even make a road in the wilderness, And rivers in the desert."

"Some of us think holding on makes us strong, but sometimes it is letting go."
- *Hermann Hesse*

PRACTICAL STEPS FOR APPLICATION:

1. Write out all offense and the people who offended you

2. Forgive and let go of it now

3. Cancel their offense you wrote as a sign of forgive and forget.

AUGUST 13

Hope and Integrity

ANCHOR SCRIPTURE: PSALM 25:21

"May integrity and uprightness protect me, because my hope, Lord, is in you."

"When I die, my integrity goes to the grave with me"
- *Ilka V. Chavez*

PRACTICAL STEPS FOR APPLICATION:

1. Develop an appetite from today to know God

2. Make up your mind to follow the way righteousness.

Journal

AUGUST 14

Why Worry?

ANCHOR SCRIPTURE: MATTHEW 6:27

"Can any one of you by worrying add a single hour to your life?" (NIV)

"Our fatigue is often caused not by work, but by worry, frustration and resentment."
– *Dale Carnegie*

PRACTICAL STEPS FOR APPLICATION:

1. Write out five things that makes you worry

2. Put those things in God's care

3. Believe God to do beyond your expectation.

Journal

AUGUST 15

Making Plans

ANCHOR SCRIPTURE: PROVERBS 19:21

"Many are the plans in a person's heart, but it is the LORD's purpose that prevails." (NIV)

"Life is what happens to us while we are making other plans."
- *Allen Saunders*

PRACTICAL STEPS FOR APPLICATION:

1. Go and share your plans for this year with mentor or trusted personnel for advice and counsel.

2. Pray and seek God for divine instruction and counsel.

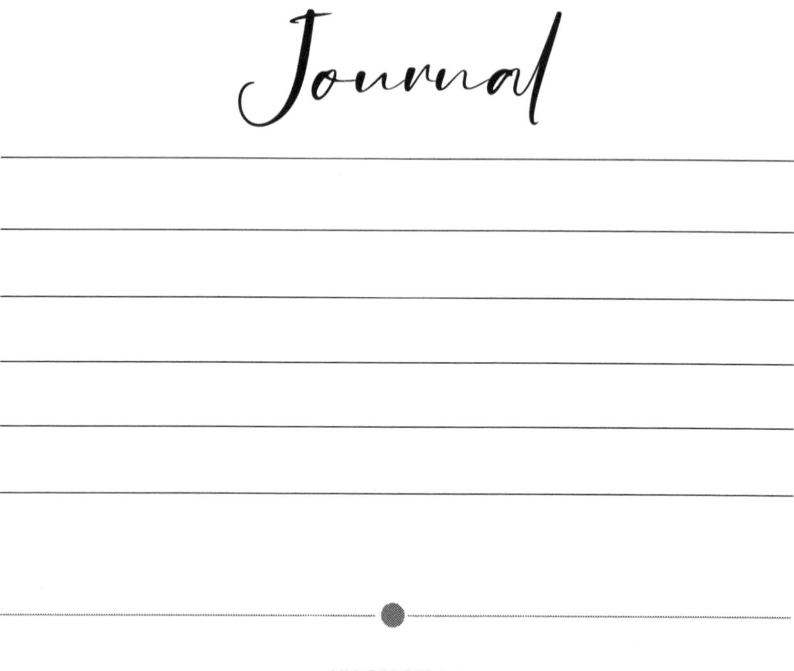

AUGUST 16

Forgive

ANCHOR SCRIPTURE: COLOSSIANS 3:13

"Bear with each other and forgive one another if any of you has a grievance against someone. Forgive as the Lord forgave you."

"I believe that life is short, and there is too much time wasted bearing grudges, and I like to move on."
- *Sam Taylor-Johnson*

PRACTICAL STEPS FOR APPLICATION:

1. Determine not to revenge the evil done against you

2. Pray and forgive your offenders today.

AUGUST 17

The Secret Ingredient

ANCHOR SCRIPTURE: 2 PETER 1:5-7 (NIV)

For this very reason, make every effort to add to your faith goodness; and to goodness, knowledge and to knowledge, self-control; and to self-control, perseverance; and to perseverance, godliness; and to godliness, mutual affection; and to mutual affection, love.

"A well-made salad must have a certain uniformity; it should make perfect sense for those ingredients to share a bowl."
-Yotam Ottolenghi

PRACTICAL STEPS FOR APPLICATION:

1. Study 2 Peter chapter one and meditate on it

2. Say to you yourself today "I have faith, goodness, knowledge, self-control, godliness. Etc.

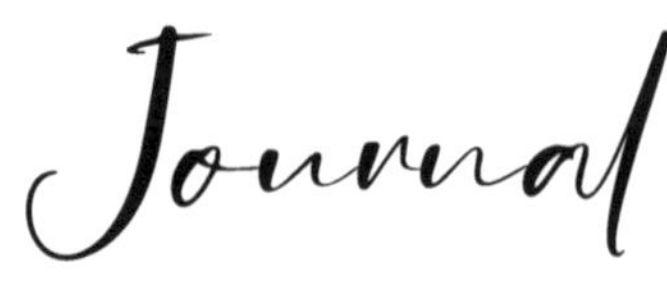

AUGUST 18

Own Your Truth

ANCHOR SCRIPTURE: JOHN 8:32

"And you will know the truth, and the truth will set you free."

"Harmony makes small things grow,
lack of it makes great things decay."
-Sallust

PRACTICAL STEPS FOR APPLICATION:

1. Look around your city find the less privilege and encourage them and bless them with substance to show love.

2. Decide to love the way Jesus loves you.

Journal

AUGUST 19

Independence

ANCHOR SCRIPTURE: 2 CORINTHIANS 3:17

"Now the Lord is the Spirit, and where the Spirit of the Lord is, there is freedom." (NIV)

"True independence and freedom can only exist in doing what's right."
-Brigham Young

PRACTICAL STEPS FOR APPLICATION:

1. Determine today to always rely on God

2. Pray to God to bring you to experiencing freedom from all oppressions.

3. Make confessions of freedom and liberty.

Journal

AUGUST 20

Using your Freedom

ANCHOR SCRIPTURE: GALATIANS 5:13

"You, my brothers and sisters, were called to be free. But do not use your freedom to indulge the flesh; rather, serve one another humbly in love." (NIV)

"If you give up your freedom for safety,
you don't deserve either one."
-Benjamin Franklin

PRACTICAL STEPS FOR APPLICATION:

1. With the knowledge of who you are in Christ decree and declare your pa h into freedom

2. Say "am above all oppressions of darkness and light and I have dominion".

3. Read and meditate on Colossians chapter one.

AUGUST 21

Cardiopulmonary Resuscitation (CPR)

ANCHOR SCRIPTURE: GALATIANS 5:13

For this is what the high and exalted One says-- he who lives forever, whose name is holy: "I live in a high and holy place, but also with the one who is contrite and lowly in spirit, to revive the spirit of the lowly and to revive the heart of the contrite. (NIV)

"Take some time to learn first aid and CPR.
It saves lives, and it works."
- *Bobby Sherman*

PRACTICAL STEPS FOR APPLICATION:

1. Read and study the book of James chapter four

2. Decide to increase your devotional time from now on.

AUGUST 22

Prioritizing

ANCHOR SCRIPTURE: MATTHEW 6:33

"But seek first his kingdom and his righteousness, and all these things will be given to you as well."

"Effective leadership is putting first things first. Effective management is discipline, carrying it out."
-Stephen Covey

PRACTICAL STEPS FOR APPLICATION:

1. Makeup your mind to put God first in all your endeavor this week and beyond.

2. Seek the will of God first before take ng any step this year.

AUGUST 23

Be Happy

ANCHOR SCRIPTURE: PSALM 37:4

Take delight in the Lord, and he will give you the desires of your heart. (NIV)"

"Your heart is where your treasure is, and you must find your treasure in order to make sense of everything."
-Paulo Coelho

PRACTICAL STEPS FOR APPLICATION:

1. Spend thirty minutes singing praise and worship with your family and friends

2. Go for a picnic today and have fun.

AUGUST 24

A Time of Rest

ANCHOR SCRIPTURE: MARK 2:27 (NLT)

"Jesus says, the Sabbath was made to meet the needs of people, and not people to meet the requirements of the Sabbath."

"There is virtue in work and there is virtue in rest.
Use both and overlook neither."
- *Alan Cohen*

PRACTICAL STEPS FOR APPLICATION:

1. Make up your mind to have a rest with your family

2. The best place to rest is in prayer therefore take time to prayer by quoting distractions

Journal

AUGUST 25

Compassion

ANCHOR SCRIPTURE: EPHESIANS 4:31-32

"Get rid of all bitterness, rage and anger, brawling and slander, along with every form of malice. Be kind and compassionate to one another, forgiving each other, just as in Christ God forgave you."

"Love and compassion are necessities, not luxuries. Without them humanity cannot survive."
-Dalai Lama

PRACTICAL STEPS FOR APPLICATION:

1. Go out today and show compassion to somebody today.

2. Share God's word with someone today

3. Pray for someone and give a gift today.

Journal

____

____

____

____

AUGUST 26

Seeking Happiness

ANCHOR SCRIPTURE: PSALM 37:4

"Take delight in the Lord, and he will give you the desires of your heart". (NIV)

Your heart is where your treasure is, and you must find your treasure in order to make sense of everything."
-Paulo Coelho

PRACTICAL STEPS FOR APPLICATION:

1. Spend your time singing songs of praise

2. Say I am courageous

3. Decide today to always smile and laugh.

AUGUST 27

God Hears Your Prayers

ANCHOR SCRIPTURE: PSALM 34:15

"The eyes of the Lord are on the righteous, and his ears are attentive to their cry" (NIV)

"Never forget the three powerful resources you always have available to you: love, prayer, and forgiveness."
- H. Jackson Brown, Jr.

PRACTICAL STEPS FOR APPLICATION:

1. Write out five of your requests in the journal below

2. Confess that I believe God hears me and can answer my prayers.

Journal

AUGUST 28

Faith vs. Feeling

ANCHOR SCRIPTURE: EPHESIANS 2:8

"For it is by grace you have been saved, through faith—and this is not from yourselves, it is the gift of God" (NIV)

It's hard to beat a person who never gives up."
- *Babe Ruth*

PRACTICAL STEPS FOR APPLICATION:

1. Determine today to live by faith not by feelings

2. Study the book of Romans chapter eight and ten.

Journal

AUGUST 29

Soul Health

ANCHOR SCRIPTURE: PSALM 23:3

"He refreshes my soul. He guides me along the right paths for his name's sake."

"Don't gain the world and lose your soul;
wisdom is better than silver or gold."
- *Bob Marley*

PRACTICAL STEPS FOR APPLICATION:

1. Take your time today to study God's word to give your health in your soul

2. Read with a gentle heart Psalm one hundred and nineteen (119).

Journal

AUGUST 30

Changing Tunes

ANCHOR SCRIPTURE: PSALM 98:1

"Oh, sing to the Lord a new song! For He has done marvelous things, His right hand and His holy arm have gained Him the victory

---

"How cruelly sweet are the echoes that start, when memory plays an old tune on the heart!"
-Eliza Cook

PRACTICAL STEPS FOR APPLICATION:

1. Ask the Lord to help to be flexible to his tune in life

2. Ask the Lord for wisdom to understand times and seasons.

Journal

AUGUST 31

Suiting Up

ANCHOR SCRIPTURE: EPHESIANS 6:11(NIV)

"Put on the full armor of God, so that you can take your stand against the devil's schemes."

"Wear your tragedies as armor, not shackles"

PRACTICAL STEPS FOR APPLICATION:

1. Study the book of Ephesians chapter ten from verse ten to twenty

2. Check your life today and decide to work on any of the armor you lack.

Journal

September

SEPTEMBER 1

Fruitful Hearing

ANCHOR SCRIPTURE: MARK 4:20 (NIV)

"Others, like seed sown on good soil, hear the word, accept it, and produce a crop-some thirty, some sixty, some a hundred times what was sown."

"We must stay connected to vine to keep bearing fruits."
- *Lailah Gifty Akita*

PRACTICAL STEPS FOR APPLICATION:

1. Confess today that am a Son of God and I believe the Word of God

2. Ask God for grace to be doer of God's word not just hearer alone.

Journal

SEPTEMBER 2

God is Love

ANCHOR SCRIPTURE: 1 JOHN 4:8 (NIV)

*"Whoever does not love does not know God,
because God is love."*

"When all fails, simply love"
- *Ilka V. Chavez*

PRACTICAL STEPS FOR APPLICATION:

1. Today decide to love to everyone despite their short comings

2. Refuse to hate and deceive.

3. Ask the Lord to pour out his love into your heart.

Journal

SEPTEMBER 3

Loving Choices

ANCHOR SCRIPTURE: 1 THESSALONIANS 5:14

"Admonish the idle, encourage the fainthearted, help the weak, be patient with them all"

"This life is for loving, sharing, learning, smiling, caring, forgiving, laughing, hugging, helping, dancing, wondering, healing, and even more loving..."
- *Steve Maraboli*

PRACTICAL STEPS FOR APPLICATION:

1. Find a friend today and encourage him\her

2. Ask the Lore to strengthen you in all your ways.

SEPTEMBER 4

More or Less

ANCHOR SCRIPTURE: JOHN 3:30 (NIV)

"He must become greater; I must become less."

"Less is more."
- Ludwig Mies van der Rohe

PRACTICAL STEPS FOR APPLICATION:

1. Surrender your life to the More afresh today and speak to the Lord that he should increase, and you should decrease as John the Baptist said.

2. Write out five things you want it to decrease in your life and confess

3. Write out four things you want it to increase in your life and confess it.

SEPTEMBER 5

Endurance

ANCHOR SCRIPTURE: HEBREWS 10:26

"If we deliberately keep on sinning after we have received the knowledge of the truth, no sacrifice for sins is left,"

"The sky is not my limit...I am."
-T.F. Hodge

PRACTICAL STEPS FOR APPLICATION:

1. In life you will face challenges that may not have a solution in the time you need but all you need is to endure therefore ask the Lord in bowing your knees in prayer to strengthen you and grant you grace to endure.

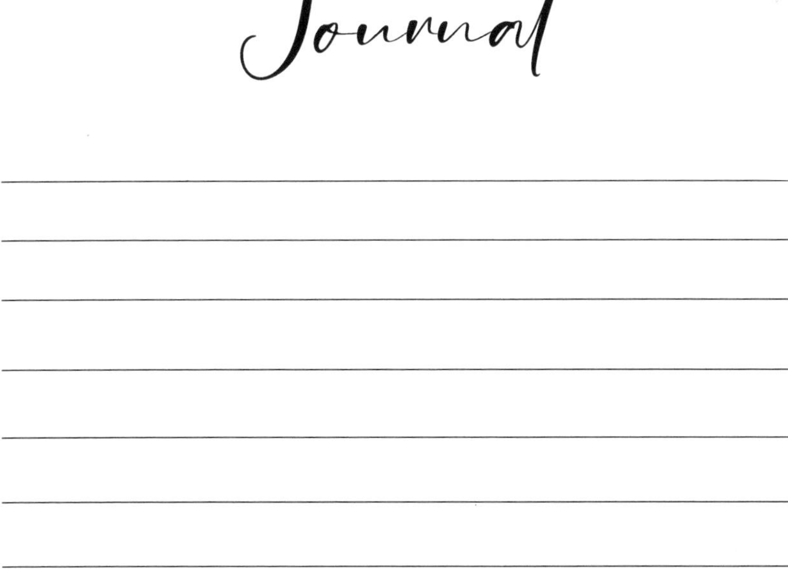

SEPTEMBER 6

Prudence

ANCHOR SCRIPTURE: PROVERBS 14:15 (NIV)

"The simple believe anything, but the prudent give thoughts to their steps."

"Wisdom at the mountain-foot sees farther than intelligence at the mountaintop."

- *Matshona Dhliwayo*

PRACTICAL STEPS FOR APPLICATION:

1. Decide to settle all your quarrel with people

2. Ask God for a simple heart.

Journal

SEPTEMBER 7

In Pursuit of Dreams

ANCHOR SCRIPTURE: MATTHEW 7:7-8 (NIV)

Ask and it will be given to you; seek and you will find; knock and the door will be opened to you. For everyone who asks receives; the one who seeks finds; and to the one who knocks, the door will be opened.

Dreams crystallize into reality when they are pursued.
- Mary Morrissey

CREATE YOUR PRACTICAL STEP(S) AND REFLECTION FOR THIS DAY.

What one thing will you do based on today's reflective devotional?

Relections

SEPTEMBER 8

Wheat and Weeds

ANCHOR SCRIPTURE: MATTHEW 13:29

"No, he answered, 'because while you are pulling the weeds, you may uproot the wheat with them."

"Until maturity, we can't tell wheat apart from weeds"

PRACTICAL STEPS FOR APPLICATION:

1. Read the parable of the sower in Matthew 13.

2. Notice the role the word of God can play in the life of s man when he prepares himself

3. Dedicate your heart to the Lord, tell him to wash it and prepare it for a visitation

SEPTEMBER 9

Thrown to the Wolves

ANCHOR SCRIPTURE: LUKE 10:3 (NIV)

"Go! I am sending you out like lambs among wolves"

"Throw me to the wolves & I'll return leading the pack"
-*Unknown*

PRACTICAL STEPS FOR APPLICATION:

1. Today, demonstrate your authority in Christ. Go out and visit people in your neighborhood, preach the gospel to them.

2. With their permission, lay hands on their sick and command the devil to leave them, them minister healing to the affected areas. Ask them to check for any level of relief, even the slightest. Repeat till they are completely healed.

Journal

SEPTEMBER 10

Wisdom and Wealth

ANCHOR SCRIPTURE: PSALM 49:20 (NIV)

"People who have wealth but lack understanding are like the beast that perish."

"The real measure of your wealth is how much you'd be worth if you lost all your money."

- *Unknown*

PRACTICAL STEPS FOR APPLICATION:

1. Read James 1:5

2. Ask the Lord to give you wisdom and help you receive it and apply it daily.

3. Be eagerly ready to supply solutions to people's problems through God's wisdom in you

Journal

SEPTEMBER 11

Help Wanted

ANCHOR SCRIPTURE: PSALM 121:2

"My help comes from the LORD, the Maker of heaven and earth."

"Always seek out the seed of triumph in every adversity."
- *Og Mandino*

PRACTICAL STEPS FOR APPLICATION:

1. Find and meditate on10 verses in the Psalms that portrays God as our helper amid trouble

2. Release help for missionaries in far and near lands. Ask that help be sent to them.

Journal

SEPTEMBER 12

Created to Create

ANCHOR SCRIPTURE: GENESIS 1:27

"So, God created mankind in his own image, in the image of God he created them; male and female he created them."

"Life isn't about finding yourself. Life is about creating yourself."
- *George Bernard Shaw*

PRACTICAL STEPS FOR APPLICATION:

1. Meditate on Genesis 1.27 -31 and 1 John 4.17

2. Begin to speak and create things you desire in your life by your words like God did.

Journal

SEPTEMBER 13

Do Not Enter

ANCHOR SCRIPTURE: PSALM 112:1 (NIV)

Praise the LORD. Blessed are those who fear the LORD, who find great delight in his commands.

"Fear God and you need not fear anyone else."
- *Woodrow Wilson*

PRACTICAL STEPS FOR APPLICATION:

1. Say "I have obtained favor with God through Christ and I am now a Son of God like Jesus, I am the blessed of God and I have been made to sit with Jesus in heavenly placed."

2. Pray for one hour today asking God for strength to be obedient.

Journal

SEPTEMBER 14

Misplaced Praise

ANCHOR SCRIPTURE: PSALM 118:28-29 (NIV)

You are my God, and I will praise you; you are my God, and I will exalt you. Give thanks to the Lord, for he is good: his love endures forever.

"Don't work for recognition but do work worthy of recognition."
- H. Jackson Brown, Jr.

PRACTICAL STEPS FOR APPLICATION:

1. Today, set aside one hour for you to engage in praises to God.

2. Be intentional to praise today with understanding

Journal

SEPTEMBER 15

Serene

ANCHOR SCRIPTURE: COLOSSIANS 3:15 (NIV)

Let the peace of Christ rule in your hearts, since as members of one body you were called to peace. And be thankful.

"Peace cannot be kept by force. It can only be achieved by understanding."
- *Albert Einstein*

PRACTICAL STEPS FOR APPLICATION:

1. Seek the peace of God in all things by making sure you always check your heart

2. Put everything that wants to steal your peace under the feet of Jesus by instantly taking it to Him in prayer.

3. Let no anger, bitterness, or resentment dwell in your hearts

Journal

SEPTEMBER 16

How is Your Faith?

ANCHOR SCRIPTURE: MATTHEW 9:22 (NIV)

Jesus turned and saw her. "Take heart, daughter," he said, "your faith has healed you." And the woman was healed at that moment.

"Worrying is arrogant because God knows what He's doing."
-Barbara Cameron

PRACTICAL STEPS FOR APPLICATION:

1. Act your faith out today, find a sick folk and lay your hands on the person, speak healing to the person and make them confirm the relief they fell

Journal

SEPTEMBER 17

Ears to Hear

ANCHOR SCRIPTURE: MARK 4:9 (NIV)

Then Jesus said, "Whoever has ears to hear, let them hear."

"Listening is a positive act: you have to put yourself out to do it."
- *David Hockney*

PRACTICAL STEPS FOR APPLICATION:

1. Go to a quiet place with a pen and a book, there pray for about 1 hour

2.Then listen to God speak to you, write out the instructions or enlightenment you get.

Journal

SEPTEMBER 18

Personal Greatness

ANCHOR SCRIPTURE: PHILIPPIANS 2:3

Do nothing out of selfish ambition or vain conceit. Rather, in humility value others above yourselves

---

"The person who clears the path ultimately controls its direction, just as the canvas shapes the painting."
- *Ryan Holiday*

PRACTICAL STEPS FOR APPLICATION:

1. Make it a duty to respect and serve others today as it lies in your capacity.

2. Do something for someone who honors you to show them that you appreciate them.

SEPTEMBER 19

Temptation

ANCHOR SCRIPTURE: HEBREWS 2:18 (NIV)

Because he himself suffered when he was tempted,
he is able to help those who are being tempted.

"Opportunity may knock once, but temptation leans on the doorbell."
- *Unknown*

PRACTICAL STEPS FOR APPLICATION:

1. In the period of Jesus' temptation, he prayed earnestly. Today, spend 3 hours in prayer, asking the Lord to strengthen you in times of trouble

Journal

SEPTEMBER 20

Stand Firm

ANCHOR SCRIPTURE: EPHESIANS 6:10

Finally, be strong in the Lord and in his mighty power.

"It is not the beauty of a building you should look at; it's the construction of the foundation that will stand the test of time."
- *David Allan Coe*

PRACTICAL STEPS FOR APPLICATION:

1. Make a list of your greatest fears, take them to the Lord and ask him to help you become strong.

Journal

SEPTEMBER 21

Parked in Pain

ANCHOR SCRIPTURE: ISAIAH 48:17 (AMPC)

Thus says the LORD, your Redeemer, the Holy One of Israel:
I am the LORD your God, who teaches you to profit,
who leads you in the way that you should go.

Your pain is not your identity. Press forward and be free. The choice is yours.

CREATE YOUR PRACTICAL STEP(S) AND REFLECTION FOR THIS DAY.

What one thing will you do based on today's reflective devotional?

Reflections

SEPTEMBER 22

Live in the Moment

ANCHOR SCRIPTURE: DANIEL 2:21 (NIV)

He changes times and seasons; he deposed kings and raises up others. He gives wisdom to the wise and knowledge to the discerning."

Be present in all things and thankful for all things."
- *Maya Angelou*

PRACTICAL STEPS FOR APPLICATION:

1. Decide to enjoy the moment and seize your opportunities

2. Plan an outing with your family members or close associates soon to cool off.

SEPTEMBER 23

Rebuild

ANCHOR SCRIPTURE: GALATIANS 2:18 (ESV)

For if I rebuild what I tore down, I prove myself to be a transgressor.

It is the neglect of timely repair that makes rebuilding necessary.
- *Richard Whately*

CREATE YOUR PRACTICAL STEP(S) AND REFLECTION FOR THIS DAY.

What one thing will you do based on today's reflective devotional?

Reflections

SEPTEMBER 24

Mistakes

1 THESSALONIANS 5:19 (NIV)

Do not quench the Spirit;

"There is nothing wrong with making mistakes,
but one should always make new ones. Repeating mistakes
is a hallmark of dim consciousness."
-Dave Sim

CREATE YOUR PRACTICAL STEP(S) AND REFLECTION FOR THIS DAY.

What one thing will you do based on today's reflective devotional?

Relections

SEPTEMBER 25

Showers of Blessings

ANCHOR SCRIPTURE: EZEKIEL 34:26

"I will make them and the places surrounding my hill a blessing. I will send down showers in season; there will be showers of blessing."

" Our prayers should be for blessings in general, for God knows best what is good for us."
- *Socrates*

PRACTICAL STEPS FOR APPLICATION:

1. Spend 1 hour in thanksgiving to God today

2. Sing, dance and get other loved ones to join you

SEPTEMBER 26

Ask

ANCHOR SCRIPTURE: JOHN 16:24(NIV)

Until now you have not asked for anything in my name. Ask and you will receive, and your joy will be complete."

"If they can get you asking the wrong questions, they don't have to worry about answers."
- *Thomas Pynchon*

PRACTICAL STEPS FOR APPLICATION:

1. Make a list of prayer requests you would like to offer

2. Read and meditate on John 16.21 then start making your requests according to the list

3. Tick the items on the list with thanksgiving as you get answers

SEPTEMBER 27

Let It Be

ANCHOR SCRIPTURE: JOHN 14:27 (ESV)

Peace I leave with you; my peace I give to you. Not as the world gives do I give to you. Let not your hearts be troubled, neither let them be afraid.

There will be an answer, let it be"
– *The Beatles."*

PRACTICAL STEPS FOR APPLICATION:

1. Today, if there is any pending case you are not letting go, in the light of the teaching today consider letting it go

2. Pray to the Lord to strengthen your heart

SEPTEMBER 28

Stay In The Ring

ANCHOR SCRIPTURE: 2 CORINTHIANS 12:9

"But he said to me, My grace is sufficient for you, for my power is made perfect in weakness. Therefore, I will boast all the more gladly about my weaknesses, so that Christ's power may rest on me."

"God doesn't cancel the fight; he gives you what it takes to win!"
- Dr. Derek Grier

PRACTICAL STEPS FOR APPLICATION:

1. Read 2 Corinthians 12

2. Pray and ask the Lord to help you remain in the game

3. Plan to increase your service to the Lord

SEPTEMBER 29

Trials are Temporary

ANCHOR SCRIPTURE: 2 CORINTHIANS 4:18 (NIV)

"So, we fix our eyes not on what is seen, but on what is unseen, since what is seen is temporary, but what is unseen is eternal."

"The closer you are to the end of your temporal trials, the louder the voice of critics. Close your ears to the heavy downpours of their discouragements. God whispers: "I am with you"!"
-Israelmore Ayivor

PRACTICAL STEPS FOR APPLICATION:

1. Spend 3 hours in prayers today about the future you want to have in the service of the Lord

2. Plan a personal retreat of more than one day and ensure you embark on it when it is possible

Journal

SEPTEMBER 30

The Truth Frees

ANCHOR SCRIPTURE: JOHN 8:32 (NIV)

"Then you will know the truth, and the truth will set you free."

"The truth was always the truth, but until I knew the truth for myself, I couldn't be free."
-Shelley Hendrix

PRACTICAL STEPS FOR APPLICATION:

1. Search for the scriptural perspectives and promises for your finance, family, career, ministry, and life.

2. Meditate on them until you believe them fully and you begin to speak them into being

October

OCTOBER 1

Enslaved by Habits

ANCHOR SCRIPTURE: 1 CORINTHIANS 6:12 ESV

"All things are lawful for me," but not all things are helpful. "All things are lawful for me," but I will not be enslaved by anything.

"Chains of habit are too light to be felt
until they are too heavy to be broken."
-Warren Buffett

PRACTICAL STEPS FOR APPLICATION:

1. Today, identify the areas of your life you have been enslaved

2. Pray for your liberation with God's word

3. See and discuss with a mentor

Journal

___

___

___

OCTOBER 2

Glow to Glow

ANCHOR SCRIPTURE: PSALM 43:3 (ESV)

*"Send out your light and your truth; let them lead me;
let them bring me to your holy hill and to your dwelling!"*

"A candle loses nothing by lighting another candle.
-James Keller

PRACTICAL STEPS FOR APPLICATION:

1. Today, begin to scout out people to mentor and help grow.

2. Once you get them begin training and encouraging them

OCTOBER 3

Reclaim Your Peace

ANCHOR SCRIPTURE: MATTHEW 10:13

*If the home is deserving, let your peace rest on it;
if it is not, let your peace return to you.*

"You can't shake hands with a clenched fist"
– *Indira Gandhi*

PRACTICAL STEPS FOR APPLICATION:

1. Identify the places where your services and help are not being appreciated

2. Check for the need of those communities and try to tailor your services to meet those needs

3. If you cannot be of help, consider withdrawing and focusing on other places

Journal

OCTOBER 4

Hands Off

ANCHOR SCRIPTURE: MATTHEW 10:13

"He says, "Be Still, and know that I am God; I will be exalted among the nations, I will be exalted in the earth"

PRACTICAL STEPS FOR APPLICATION:

1. Read Psalm 46

2. Decide to address concerns from the standpoint of the spirit of God first

3. Spend time thanking God today

Journal

OCTOBER 5

Limited Vision

ANCHOR SCRIPTURE: EPHESIANS 1:18-20

PRACTICAL STEPS FOR APPLICATION:

1. Reflect on how God has helped you in the past to have your visions come through in times past

2. Begin to outline your vision for the future and ask God again to help you achieve them

Journal

OCTOBER 6

A Clean Slate

ANCHOR SCRIPTURE: PSALM 32:5 (NLT)

Finally, I confessed all my sins to you and stopped trying to hide my guilt. I said to myself, "I will confess my rebellion to the Lord." And you forgave me! All my guilt is gone.

PRACTICAL STEPS FOR APPLICATION:

1. Read Psalm 32

2. Make your slate clean, confess your faults and make the records straight. Where possible, make restitution and rebuild broken relationships.

Journal

OCTOBER 7

To Judge Or To Love...

ANCHOR SCRIPTURE: GALATIANS 6:1 (NIV)

Brothers and sisters, if someone is caught in a sin, you who live by the Spirit should restore that person gently. But watch yourselves, or you also may be tempted.

An individual has not started living until he can rise above the narrow confines of his individualistic concerns to the broader concerns of all humanity.
- *Martin Luther King, Jr.*

PRACTICAL STEPS FOR APPLICATION:

1. Reflect on how you have handled all previous interactions to know if you judged them or you showed love

2. Make a commitment to always take the path of love in your interactions with your tribe, no matter how diverse they are or what kind of mistake they make.

OCTOBER 8

Embrace Your Power

ANCHOR SCRIPTURE: PSALM 139:14 (NIV)

"I praise you because I am fearfully and wonderfully made. your works are wonderful, I know that full well"

"No one is you and that is your power."
-Anonymous

PRACTICAL STEPS FOR APPLICATION:

1. Write out ten areas in your life you enjoy massive strength

2. Appreciate God for the unique abilities in you

3. Look for a way to put your greatest potentials into expression today

OCTOBER 9

Ignite your Day

ANCHOR SCRIPTURE: JOHN 8:12

"Then Jesus again spoke to them, saying, "I am the Light of the world; he who follows Me will not walk in the darkness, but will have the Light of life."

"Just in case no one told you today... You are good enough."

PRACTICAL STEPS FOR APPLICATION:

1. Look for ways to be the light that others need to live today and walk to display to them the life of Jesus

2. Help someone discover and live their light today

3. Ask the Lord to bring people you can be a blessing to your way

Journal

OCTOBER 10

Up Level Your Thinking

ANCHOR SCRIPTURE: PSALM 19:14 (ESV)

Let the words of my mouth and the meditation of my heart be acceptable in your sight, O Lord, my rock, and my redeemer.

"You have the capacity to leave a lasting impact and indelible impression upon this world.... Claim the sacred spaces of your minds, nurture and cultivate a vision of fulfillment, and move toward that destiny with patience, perseverance, and prayer."
-Mahershala Ali

PRACTICAL STEPS FOR APPLICATION:

1. Read Philippians 4.8

2. Decide to live an excellent life from today.

OCTOBER 11

Help Others Win

ANCHOR SCRIPTURE: JOHN 3:30

"He must become greater; I must become less."

"The way to achieve your own success is to be willing to help somebody else get it first."
-Iyanla Vanzant

PRACTICAL STEPS FOR APPLICATION:

1. Find a mentee to help become better at what he does by training him with the lessons you have learnt

2. Go out and preach the gospel to someone, when you make a convert, teach them till they can teach others about God

OCTOBER 12

Disappointment

ANCHOR SCRIPTURE: 1 PETER 5:6-8

"So humble yourselves under the mighty power of God, and at the right time he will lift you up in honor. Give all your worries and cares to God, for he cares about you. Stay alert! Watch out for your great enemy, the devil. He prowls around like a roaring lion, looking for someone to devour."

"Blessed is he who expects nothing, for he shall never be disappointed."
-Alexander Pope

PRACTICAL STEPS FOR APPLICATION:

1. Leave all associations and company that seeks to emphasis your problems over the work of Christ for you

2. Spend one hour in prayer today

OCTOBER 13

Serenity- The Power of Peace

ANCHOR SCRIPTURE: COLOSSIANS 3:15

Let the peace of Christ rule in your hearts since as members of one body you were called to peace and be thankful."

"You are called to peace, be grateful"

PRACTICAL STEPS FOR APPLICATION:

1. Make a list of the things that trouble you classify them under two subheadings; one for those you can change, the other for those you cannot change

2. While you stop being worried about the things you cannot change, start learning of how you can change the things you can

Journal

OCTOBER 14

Flow Versus Force

ANCHOR SCRIPTURE: PHILIPPIANS 2:13

"That energy is God's energy, an energy deep within you, God himself willing and working at what will give him the most pleasure.

"May what I do flow from me like a river, no forcing and no holding back, the way it is with children."
-Rainer Maria Rilke

PRACTICAL STEPS FOR APPLICATION:

1. Examine yourself and your leadership note three places you may be struggling

2. Ask God to show you the natural part of you that will be the answer to the problems

OCTOBER 15

Blessed

ANCHOR SCRIPTURE: PHILIPPIANS 2:13

Blessed is the one who does not walk in step with the wicked or stand in the way that sinners take or sit in the company of mockers, but whose delight is in the law of the Lord, and who meditates on his law day and night. That person is like a tree planted by streams of water, which yields its fruit in season and whose leaf does not wither— whatever they do prospers"

"Blessed are they who see beautiful things in humble places where other people see nothing."
- *Camille Pissarro*

PRACTICAL STEPS FOR APPLICATION:

1. Read and declare Psalm One boldly and personalize the blessings in it based on the works of Jesus

OCTOBER 16

What Do You Think?

ANCHOR SCRIPTURE: MATTHEW 6:21

"For where your treasure is, there your heart will be also"

"Leading from your heart doesn't diminish your power.
It is your power.
- *Christine Arylo*

PRACTICAL STEPS FOR APPLICATION:

1. As a leader, think of a way to give people under you an avenue to express their potentials

2. Begin learning a new skill, it could be a new language or a musical skill etc.

Journal

OCTOBER 17

Observe vs. Watch

ANCHOR SCRIPTURE: HABAKKUK 1:5 (CSB)

"Look at the nations and observe--be utterly astounded! For I am doing something in your days that you will not believe when you hear about it."

To sail successfully, you need to observe with great care. You need to identify what the wind and the water are telling you and then find a way to execute, to reach whatever goal you've set, be that simply making it home or winning a race.

-Diane Greene

PRACTICAL STEPS FOR APPLICATION:

1. Today, as you go about your daily duties, determine to be more observant about things around you such as yourself, your coworkers, family and so on. Write down the differences you noticed but were not aware of until you started consciously observing in your journal

Journal

OCTOBER 18

Leading with Courage

ANCHOR SCRIPTURE: JOSHUA 1:9

"Have I not commanded you? Be strong and courageous. Do not be afraid; do not be discouraged, for the lord your God will be with you wherever you go.

Courage is not the lack of fear, it is acting despite the fear

---

PRACTICAL STEPS FOR APPLICATION:

1. Read the story of the leadership of Joshua

2. Pray and ask the Lord to teach you courage by himself

Journal

OCTOBER 19

Blessings or Curses

ANCHOR SCRIPTURE: DEUTERONOMY 30:19 (NLT)

Today I have given you the choice between life and death, between blessings and curses. Now I call on heaven and earth to witness the choice you make. Oh, that you would choose life, so that you and your descendants might live!

"What you focus on grows, what you think about expands, and what you dwell upon determines your destiny."
- *Robin S.*

PRACTICAL STEPS FOR APPLICATION:

1. Don't be in a rush to make decisions. Take time to think things through, and irrespective of the seeming challenges, always make the choice that leads toward life

OCTOBER 20

Stay the Course

ANCHOR SCRIPTURE: HEBREWS 12:1-2 (ESV)

Therefore, since we are surrounded by so great a cloud of witnesses, let us also lay aside every weight, and sin which clings so closely, and let us run with endurance the race that is set before us, looking to Jesus, the founder and perfecter of our faith, who for the joy that was set before him endured the cross, despising the shame, and is seated at the right hand of the throne of God.

"The only way to finish is to stay the course."
- Ilka V. Chavez

PRACTICAL STEPS FOR APPLICATION:

1. In order not to get overwhelmed, when problems arise, take time off to recharge your faith batteries and seek wisdom. You will give up more easily when you get overwhelmed. Solve problems one at a time.

Here is a special invitation for you. If you have not declared Jesus Lord as your savior, here is your opportunity to do so. Romans 10:9-11 says, if you declare with your mouth, "Jesus is Lord," and believe in your heart that God raised him for the dead, you will be saved. For it is with your heart that you believe and are justified, and it is with your mouth that process your faith and are saved. For the Scripture says, WHOEVER BELIEVES IN HIM WILL NOT BE DISAPPOINTED."

If you declare this, please reply Amen. Welcome back to the family, welcome home!

Journal

OCTOBER 21

Seize the Moment

ANCHOR SCRIPTURE: EPHESIANS 5: 15-17 (MSG)

"So, watch your step. Use your head. Make the most of every chance you get. These are desperate times! Don't live carelessly, unthinkingly. Make sure you understand what the Master wants."

"Stop acting as if life is a rehearsal. Live this day as if it were your last. The past is over and gone. The future is not guaranteed. "
- *Wayne Dyer*

PRACTICAL STEPS FOR APPLICATION:

1. Do you let opportunities pass you by? Stop it! Another opportunity will come your way soon, jump at it, even if you fail, you will learn.

2. Carry out an inner search to know the reasons why you avoid taking advantage of opportunities. Is it fear, laziness, or low self-esteem? Whatever it is, determine to overcome it and step out.

OCTOBER 22

Mistakes

ANCHOR SCRIPTURE: 1 THESSALONIANS 5:19 (NIV)

"Do not quench the Spirit;"

"There is nothing wrong with making mistakes,
but one should always make new ones. Repeating mistakes
is a hallmark of dim consciousness."
-Dave Sim

PRACTICAL STEPS FOR APPLICATION:

1. In every situation you make a mistake, learn to implement Ms. Boy's advice

2. Listen to the Holy Spirit more. He knows ALL things and He can lead you into the right path and you won't make any mistake. If you do not have Him, tell Jesus to baptize you now and He will

OCTOBER 23

Readiness

ANCHOR SCRIPTURE: PROVERBS 13:10

"Where there is strife, there is pride, but wisdom is found in those who take advice.

"When the student is ready the teacher appears.
When the student is truly ready the teacher disappears."
- *Lao Tzu*

PRACTICAL STEPS FOR APPLICATION:

1. Always be ready and prepared to dish out wisdom to your tribe by constantly knowledge yourself

Journal

OCTOBER 24

Freed by Grace

ANCHOR SCRIPTURE: ROMANS 7:6

"But now, by dying to what once bound us, we have been released from the law so that we serve in the new way of the Spirit, and not in the old way of the written code."

"Grace is the voice that calls us to change and then gives us the power to pull it off."
– *Max Lucado*

PRACTICAL STEPS FOR APPLICATION:

1. On one hand, know that as a human, you are limited and weak in some areas. But as a believing leader, KNOW that it was for that reason Christ came to give you grace to be strong in weakness.

2. Now anytime you encounter weakness, tap into the grace of God, and use it to overcome.

Journal

OCTOBER 25

All My Children

ANCHOR SCRIPTURE: 1 JOHN 3:1 (NIV)

See what great love the Father has lavished on us, that we should be called children of God! And that is what we are! The reason the world does not know us is that it did not know him.

"What it's like to be a parent: It's one of the hardest things you'll ever do but in exchange it teaches you the meaning of unconditional love."
-Nicholas Sparks

PRACTICAL STEPS FOR APPLICATION:

1. Take a step back today to ruminate on and appreciate God the Father for the endless love He has lavished on you and your tribe.

Journal

OCTOBER 26

Trust

ANCHOR SCRIPTURE: PSALM 56:9-11 (ESV)

"Then my enemies will turn back in the day when I call. This I know, that God is for me. In God, whose word I praise, in the Lord, whose word I praise, in God I trust; I shall not be afraid. What can man do to me?"

" Never be afraid to trust an unknown future to a known God."
-Corrie ten Boom

PRACTICAL STEPS FOR APPLICATION:

1. Read and memorize the anchor scripture for today alongside Proverbs 3:5-6

2. God manages the whole world, He cannot mismanage your life, learn to trust Him in all things

Journal

OCTOBER 27

Teachable

ANCHOR SCRIPTURE: PSALM 32:8- (NIV)

*"I will instruct you and teach you in the way you should go;
I will counsel you with my loving eye on you."*

"If you are not willing to learn, no one can help you.
If you are determined to learn, no one can stop you."
-Zig Ziglar

PRACTICAL STEPS FOR APPLICATION:

1. Before your tribe becomes teachable, are you also teachable? Learn to be teachable, they will fall in line too very soon

2. Be patient with the unteachable ones, let them build their trust in your first, then they will find it easier to be led by you.

OCTOBER 28

Stewardship

ANCHOR SCRIPTURE: PHILIPPIANS 3:12 (NLT)

"I don't mean to say that I have already achieved these things or that I have already reached perfection. But I press on to possess that perfection for which Christ Jesus first possessed me."

"A leader must be a good listener. He must be willing to take counsel. He must show a genuine concern and love for those under his stewardship."

- James E. Faust

PRACTICAL STEPS FOR APPLICATION:

1. Wait on God to receive more grace to be a worthy steward

2. Don't serve and lead your tribe alone, teach them to be good stewards too

Journal

OCTOBER 29

Learn it. Live it. Lead it.

ANCHOR SCRIPTURE: PHILIPPIANS 4:9 (NIV)

"Whatever you have learned or received or heard from me or seen in me—put it into practice. And the God of peace will be with you."

"The past is where you learned the lesson. The future is where you apply the lesson, don't give up in the middle."
~ *Dhiraj Raj*

PRACTICAL STEPS FOR APPLICATION:

1. Celebrate everything in your life, whether good or bad. Good because you did well, bad because you learnt something new.

2. Review the bad things so you can make the most of the lesson and do better next time

Journal

OCTOBER 30

Diligence

ANCHOR SCRIPTURE: 1 TIMOTHY 4:15–16 (NIV)

"Be diligent in these matters; give yourself wholly to them, so that everyone may see your progress. Watch your life and doctrine closely. Persevere in them, because if you do, you will save both yourself and your hearers."

The expectations of life depend upon diligence; the mechanic that would perfect his work must first sharpen his tools.
-Confucius

PRACTICAL STEPS FOR APPLICATION:

1. Learn to go the extra mile in leading your tribe the right way

2. Do not despair in the face of seeming unfruitfulness, remain diligent and you will be rewarded

OCTOBER 31

Open Doors

ANCHOR SCRIPTURE: REVELATIONS 3:7 (NIV)

"To the angel of the church in Philadelphia write: These are the words of him who is holy and true, who holds the key of David. What he opens no one can shut, and what he shuts no one can open."

"Personality can open doors, but only an upright character keeps them open."
-Elmer G. Letterman

PRACTICAL STEPS FOR APPLICATION:

1. Audit your character to make sure it models what you will like your tribe to be

2. Ensure you set an example of a good character, filled with love and compassion in your interactions with others

Journal

NOVEMBER 1

Sacrifice

ANCHOR SCRIPTURE: JOHN 15:13 (TPT)

*"For the greatest love of all is a love that sacrifices all.
And this great love is demonstrated when
a person sacrifices his life for his friends"*

---

*"Sacrifice is a part of life. It's supposed to be.
It's not something to regret. It's something*

PRACTICAL STEPS FOR APPLICATION:

1. Call an old friend or family member who you have not talked to in sometime.

2. Today, go the extra mile in loving those around you.

Journal

NOVEMBER 2

Unwavering

ANCHOR SCRIPTURE: ISAIAH 40:31 (AMP)

"But those who wait for the Lord [who expect, look for, and hope in Him] Will gain new strength and renew their power; They will lift up their wings [and rise up close to God] like eagles [rising toward the sun]; They will run and not become weary, They will walk and not grow tired."

"Once you are clear about what you wish to create, you can maintain a steady stream of thoughts – unwavering, resolute, and focused."
-Dr Prem Jagyasi

PRACTICAL STEPS FOR APPLICATION:

1. Endeavor to wait upon the lord daily in praying and studying his word.

2. Believe you can always make it even amid difficulty, believe in yourself.

Journal

NOVEMBER 3

Happy International Mother's Day to all Moms!

ANCHOR SCRIPTURE: PROVERBS 31:31 (NIV)

"Honor her for all that her hands have done, and let her works bring her praise at the city gate."

"Motherhood is a choice you make every day, to put someone else's happiness and well-being ahead of your own, to teach the hard lessons, to do the right thing even when you're not sure what the right thing is...and to forgive yourself, over and over again, for doing everything wrong."

\- *Donna Ball*

CREATE YOUR PRACTICAL STEP(S) AND REFLECTION FOR THIS DAY.

What one thing will you do based on today's reflective devotional?

Reflections

NOVEMBER 4

Inner Peace (Peace of Mind)

ANCHOR SCRIPTURE: JOHN 14:27 (AMP)

Peace I leave with you; My [perfect] peace I give to you; not as the world gives do I give to you. Do not let your heart be troubled, nor let it be afraid. [Let My perfect peace calms you in every circumstance and give you courage and s trength for every challenge.]

"Peace is the result of retraining your mind to process life as it is, rather than as you think it should be."
-Wayne W. Dyer

CREATE YOUR PRACTICAL STEP(S) AND REFLECTION FOR THIS DAY.

What one thing will you do based on today's reflective devotional?

Relections

NOVEMBER 5

Orchestrate

ANCHOR SCRIPTURE: COLOSSIANS 1:17

He is before all things, and in him all things hold together.

"The perfect orchestration of the symphony of life is one of the Creator's greatest and most beautiful miracles."
-Suzy Kassem

PRACTICAL STEPS FOR APPLICATION:

1. Submit yourself to the lord's direction in that situation that look complicating by acting based on his word.

Journal

NOVEMBER 6

When Scared Love

ANCHOR SCRIPTURE: 1 JOHN 4:18

There is no fear in love. But perfect love drives out fear because fear has to do with punishment. The one who fears is not made perfect in love.

If light is love, then fear is its shadow
- *L.J. Vanier*

PRACTICAL STEPS FOR APPLICATION:

1. Read through the book of psalm 23 and declare the promise of the lord.

2. Live with the consciousness of the love God has for you.

Journal

NOVEMBER 7

The Road Less Traveled

ANCHOR SCRIPTURE: ISAIAH 26:3 - (AMP)

"You will keep in perfect and constant peace the one whose mind is steadfast [that is, committed and focused on You—in both inclination and character], Because he trusts and takes refuge in You [with hope and confident expectation]."

"Two roads diverged in a wood and I - I took the one less traveled by, and that has made all the difference."
- *Robert Frost*

PRACTICAL STEPS FOR APPLICATION:

1. Ask the lord for direction and courage to journey through to the end.

2. Write down decisions that help you accomplish well in this journey.

Journal

NOVEMBER 8

Extravagant Love

ANCHOR SCRIPTURE: 1 JOHN 4:10

"This is love: not that we loved God, but that he loved us and sent his Son as an atoning sacrifice for our sins."

"That's what love does- It pursues blindly, unflinchingly, and without end. Even if it costs everything."
- *Bob Goff*

PRACTICAL STEPS FOR APPLICATION:

1. Forgive those who offend you and are not ready to reconcile.

2. Tell people around you about the extravagant love of God for them.

Journal

NOVEMBER 9

Extra Grace Required (EGR)

ANCHOR SCRIPTURE: COLOSSIANS 3:13- (AMP)

"Bearing graciously with one another, and willingly forgiving each other if one has a cause for complaint against another; just as the Lord has forgiven you, so should you forgive."

"A thought to help us through these difficult times: Be kind, for everyone you meet is fighting a hard battle."
-Ian MacLaren

PRACTICAL STEPS FOR APPLICATION:

1. Write down areas of your life that require extra grace.

2. Take it to the lord in prayers

Journal

NOVEMBER 10

The Gift of Hope

ANCHOR SCRIPTURE: HEBREWS 6:19 (AMP)

"This hope [this confident assurance] we have as an anchor of the soul [it cannot slip and it cannot break down under whatever pressure bears upon it]—a safe and steadfast hope that enters within the veil [of the heavenly temple, that most Holy Place in which the very presence of God dwells]"

"The greatest gift leaders can give their people is HOPE"
- *Unknown*

PRACTICAL STEPS FOR APPLICATION:

1. Write down or see your own expected outcome in the areas where you are losing hope on.

2. Declare this boldly "I can't be hopeless I am full of hope"

NOVEMBER 11

Devoted to Prayer

ANCHOR SCRIPTURE: COLOSSIANS 4:2 (AMP)

Be persistent and devoted to prayer, being alert and focused on your prayer life with an attitude of thanksgiving.

"Our prayers may be awkward. Our attempts may be feeble. But since the power of prayer is in the one who hears it and not in the one who says it, our prayers do make a difference."
- *Max Lucado*

CREATE YOUR PRACTICAL STEP(S) AND REFLECTION FOR THIS DAY.

What one thing will you do based on today's reflective devotional?

Relections

NOVEMBER 12

Fear or Faith? The choice is yours

ANCHOR SCRIPTURE: ISAIAH 41:10 (MSG)

"Don't panic. I'm with you. There's no need to fear for I'm your God. I'll give you strength. I'll help you. I'll hold you steady, keep a firm grip on you."

There are two primary forces in this world, fear, and faith. Fear can move you to destructiveness or sickness or failure. Only in rare instances will it motivate you to accomplishment. But faith is a greater force. Faith can drive itself into your consciousness and set you free from fear forever
-Norman Vincent Peale

PRACTICAL STEPS FOR APPLICATION:

1. Speak to that situation that you are afraid of dealing with right now.

2. React to your fear by declaring God's truth about this situation.

NOVEMBER 13

Preparation

ANCHOR SCRIPTURE: PROVERBS 6:6-8 NASB

Go to the ant, O sluggard, observe her ways and be wise, which, having no chief, officer or ruler, prepares her food in the summer and gathers her provision in the harvest."

"Success is where preparation and opportunity meet."
-Bobby Unser

PRACTICAL STEPS FOR APPLICATION:

1. Create time every day to prepare for the next day.

2. Right now, prepare for the next important event of your life.

Journal

NOVEMBER 14

Humility

ANCHOR SCRIPTURE: PROVERBS 22:4

Humility is the fear of the Lord; its wages are riches and honor and life."

Mastery begins with humility.
-Robin Sharma

PRACTICAL STEPS FOR APPLICATION:

1. Remind yourself always that all you have was given to you.

2. Ask God for grace to be humble

Journal

NOVEMBER 15

Victory Walk

ANCHOR SCRIPTURE: PSALM 37:23-24 (NIV)

The Lord makes firm the steps of the one who delights in him; though he may stumble, he will not fall, for the Lord upholds him with his hand.

Once you hear the details of victory,
it is hard to distinguish it from a defeat.
- *Jean-Paul Sartre*

PRACTICAL STEPS FOR APPLICATION:

1. Declare the victory Jesus has won for you on the cross. Victory is already yours!

2. Research and practice the word of God that talk about the victory you require.

NOVEMBER 16

Ears Wide Open

ANCHOR SCRIPTURE: ISAIAH 50:4 (AMP)

"The Lord God has given Me [His [a]Servant] the tongue of disciples [as One who is taught], That I may know how to sustain the weary with a word. He awakens Me morning by morning; He awakens My ear to listen as a disciple [as One who is taught]."

Keep your eyes and ears wide open— and your mouth closed if you wish to acquire the habit of prompt decision.
- *Napoleon Hill*

PRACTICAL STEPS FOR APPLICATION:

1. Read and declare Psalm One boldly and personalize the blessings in it based on the works of Jesus

Journal

NOVEMBER 17

Redemption

ANCHOR SCRIPTURE: EPHESIANS 1:7 (AMP)

"In Him we have redemption [that is, our deliverance and salvation] through His blood, [which paid the penalty for our sin and resulted in] the forgiveness and complete pardon of our sin, in accordance with the riches of His grace."

Redemption is not perfection.
The redeemed must realize their imperfections.
- *John Piper*

PRACTICAL STEPS FOR APPLICATION:

1. Write down the area of your life that you still struggle with and look for the scripture that speak about it, read, and declare it out boldly.

2. Take (5) minutes to praise the lord for redeeming you from the power of darkness into his glorious light.

Journal

____

____

____

____

____

NOVEMBER 18

Unshakable

ANCHOR SCRIPTURE: HEBREWS 12:27 (NLT)

Therefore, since we are surrounded by so great a cloud of witnesses, let us also lay aside every weight, and sin which clings so closely, and let us run with endurance the race that is set before us, looking to Jesus, the founder and perfecter of our faith, who for the joy that was set before him endured the cross, despising the shame, and is seated at the right hand of the throne of God.

"Those who have not found their true wealth, which is the radiant joy of being and the deep, unshakable peace that comes with it, are beggars, even if they have great material wealth. They are looking outside for scraps of pleasure or fulfillment, for validation, security, or love, while they have a treasure within that not only includes all those things but is infinitely greater than anything the world can offer. "

-Eckhart Tolle

PRACTICAL STEPS FOR APPLICATION:

1. Read psalm 125 and mediate on it.

2. Write down your meditations in the journal

Journal

NOVEMBER 19

Perfect Peace

ANCHOR SCRIPTURE: ISAIAH 26:3 (NKJV)

"You will keep him in perfect peace, whose mind is stayed on You, because he trusts in You."

"Peace cannot be kept by force.
It can only be achieved by understanding."
-Albert Einstein

PRACTICAL STEPS FOR APPLICATION:

1. Take (5) minute in a solely place and think on the goodness and faithful of God.

2. Give attention to the Holy Spirit within you.

Journal

NOVEMBER 20

Give Goodness

ANCHOR SCRIPTURE: PSALM 23:6

Surely, goodness and mercy shall follow me all the days of my life, and I shall dwell in the house of the Lord forever.

"Life is an echo. What you send out, comes back. What you sow, you reap. What you give, you get. What you see in others, exists in you. Remember, life is an echo. It always gets back to you.
So, give goodness."
-*Unknown*

PRACTICAL STEPS FOR APPLICATION:

1. Pick (5) people and pray for their well- being.

2. Help someone to carry out part of his duty today.

NOVEMBER 21

Patience

ANCHOR SCRIPTURE: GALATIANS 6:9

"Let's not get tired of doing what is good, for at the right time we will reap a harvest—if we do not give up."

"Patience, persistence and perspiration make an unbeatable combination for success."
- *Napoleon Hill*

PRACTICAL STEPS FOR APPLICATION:

1. Ask the Holy Spirit to teach your patience in the place of prayer by waiting on him for 20 minutes.

2. Practice again what you are weary of doing that is right.

NOVEMBER 22

Gentleness

ANCHOR SCRIPTURE: PHILIPPIANS 4:5 (AMP)

"Let your gentle spirit [your graciousness, unselfishness, mercy, tolerance, and patience] be known to all people. The Lord is near."

I learned that it is the weak who are cruel, and that gentleness is to be expected only from the strong.

-Leo Rosten

PRACTICAL STEPS FOR APPLICATION:

1. Speak kindly to people around and do not use derogatory words.

2. Stay quiet when you are not asked to say or contribute to a matter.

Journal

NOVEMBER 23

Love Love

ANCHOR SCRIPTURE: 1 JOHN 4:7 (AMP)

"Beloved, let us [unselfishly] love and seek the best for one another, for love is from God; and everyone who loves [others] is born of God and knows God [through personal experience]

The ultimate lesson all of us have to learn is unconditional love, which includes not only others but ourselves as well.

- Elisabeth Kubler-Ross

PRACTICAL STEPS FOR APPLICATION:

1. Tell someone who hurt you, I love you because Christ love me even when am a sinner.

2. Pray for those you know hates you and forgive them.

3. Call those you have offended and seek to reconcile.

Journal

NOVEMBER 24

Faithfulness

ANCHOR SCRIPTURE: 1 THESSALONIANS 5:24 (AMP)

Faithful and absolutely trustworthy is He who is calling you [to Himself for your salvation], and He will do it [He will fulfill His call by making you holy, guarding you, watching over you, and protecting you as His own].

Health is the greatest gift, contentment the greatest wealth, faithfulness the best relationship.
- *Buddha*

PRACTICAL STEPS FOR APPLICATION:

1. Identify areas of your life that you are not faithful in and ask the holy spirt for help.

2. Keep to your word's and promise to God and to your fellow one's.

3. Confess this word "I am faithful in the name of Jesus".

Journal

NOVEMBER 25

Joy

ANCHOR SCRIPTURE: PSALM 16:11- (NIV)

"You make known to me the path of life; you will fill me with joy in your presence, with eternal pleasures at your right hand."

"If you carry joy in your heart, you can heal any moment."
-Carlos Santana

PRACTICAL STEPS FOR APPLICATION:

1. Preach to a soul about Christ today.

2. Stay in God's presence with prayer's, worship, and the scripture.

3. Smile throughout today as sign of joy in your heart.

Journal

NOVEMBER 26

Self-Control

ANCHOR SCRIPTURE: PROVERBS 25:28 (NIV)

"Like a city whose walls are broken through is a person who lacks self-control."

"Self-control is the chief element in self-respect, and self-respect is the chief element in courage."
-Thucydides

PRACTICAL STEPS FOR APPLICATION:

1. Take action base on the word of God and the description of the Holy Spirit.

2. Ask relevant questions before taking a step.

Journal

NOVEMBER 27

Kindness

ANCHOR SCRIPTURE: EPHESIANS 4:32

"Be kind and compassionate to one another, forgiving each other, just as in Christ God forgave you."

"Kindness in words creates confidence. Kindness in thinking creates profoundness. Kindness in giving creates love."
-Lao Tzu

PRACTICAL STEPS FOR APPLICATION:

1. Treat people around you like yourself.

2. Let go of offense.

Journal

NOVEMBER 28

The Beauty of Grace

ANCHOR SCRIPTURE: JOHN 1:16 (ESV)

"For from his fullness we have all received, grace upon grace..."

Grace isn't a little prayer you chant before receiving a meal.
It's a way to live. The law tells me how crooked I am.
Grace comes along and straightens me out.
- *Dwight Lyman Moody*

PRACTICAL STEPS FOR APPLICATION:

1. Continual fellowship with God and the holy spirit via prayer and the word.

2. Confess all unrighteousness in and around your life.

Journal

NOVEMBER 29

Gratitude Changes Everything

ANCHOR SCRIPTURE: 1 TIMOTHY 4:4-5 (ESV)

"For everything created by God is good, and nothing is to be rejected if it is received with thanksgiving, for it is made holy by the word of God and prayer."

"Gratitude is a spiritual force that empowers you to scale higher. You can't change to higher level without it."
- Bishop Dr. Julius Soyinka

PRACTICAL STEPS FOR APPLICATION:

1. Write down (5) things you know you would not have done by yourself that God has done and intensively appreciate him for it.

2. Call and text those who has done something for you in the past and thank them for it.

NOVEMBER 30

Lean Not On Your Own Understanding

ANCHOR SCRIPTURE: PROVERBS 3:5-6

"Trust in the LORD with all your heart; and lean not on your own understanding. In all thy ways acknowledge him, and he shall direct thy paths."

"Your mind is finite, lean not on it."
- *Loraine Angela Dixon*

PRACTICAL STEPS FOR APPLICATION:

1. Believe the word of God that he has spoken to you by acting on it.

2. Follow God's prescription of doing things.

3. Take advice and corrections.

December

DECEMBER 1

Idols in Your Heart

ANCHOR SCRIPTURE: EZEKIEL 14:3 (NLT)

Son of man, these leaders have set up idols in their hearts. They have embraced things that will make them fall into sin. Why should I listen to their requests?

"People worship what they value most."
-Pastor Jimmy Rollins

PRACTICAL STEPS FOR APPLICATION:

1. Confess to the father about any form of idol that has preoccupied your heart.

2. Go on a retreat.

Journal

DECEMBER 2

Change the Channel

ANCHOR SCRIPTURE: PHILIPPIANS 4:8(NIV)

Finally, brothers and sisters, whatever is true, whatever is noble, whatever is right, whatever is pure, whatever is lovely, whatever is admirable—if anything is excellent or praiseworthy—think about such things.

"What you focus on grows, what you think about expands, and what you dwell upon determines your destiny."
- *Robin S. Sharma*

PRACTICAL STEPS FOR APPLICATION:

1. Allow the word of the lord to regulate your thinking.

2. Staying far from people that speak negatively and think evil.

Journal

DECEMBER 3

Serve One Another

ANCHOR SCRIPTURE: 1 PETER 4:10 (ESV)

"As each has received a gift, use it to serve one another, as good stewards of God's varied grace"

"Life's most persistent and urgent question is,
'What are you doing for others?'"
- *Dr. Martin Luther King, Jr.*

PRACTICAL STEPS FOR APPLICATION:

1. Find someone who is ahead of you and serve him in your enabled capacities.

2. Submit to those that are ahead of you.

Journal

DECEMBER 4

Being Vulnerable

ANCHOR SCRIPTURE: HEBREWS 12:1-2 (ESV)

"I came to you in weakness and fear, and with much trembling and my speech and my message were not in plausible words of wisdom, but in demonstration of the Spirit and of power.

Vulnerability is the language of the soul and the voice of the heart.
- *Virginia Burges*

PRACTICAL STEPS FOR APPLICATION:

1. Ask God for help in your vulnerable state.

2. Rejoice in God's strength.

Journal

DECEMBER 5

Seek Wisdom

ANCHOR SCRIPTURE: PROVERBS 4:6 (NIV)

Do not forsake wisdom, and she will protect you;
love her, and she will watch over you.

Don't gain the world and lose your soul;
wisdom is better than silver or gold.
-Bob Marley

PRACTICAL STEPS FOR APPLICATION:

1. Wait in the place of prayer to receive wisdom and understanding.

2. Stay away from evil and take on the fear of the lord.

Journal

DECEMBER 6

Habit of Trust

ANCHOR SCRIPTURE: ISAIAH 26:4

"Trust in the LORD forever, for the LORD GOD is an everlasting rock."

"When the trust account is high, communication is easy, instant, and effective."
- *Stephen R. Covey*

PRACTICAL STEPS FOR APPLICATION:

1. Know the word of God and put your trust on them.

2. Look away from other alternative.

3. Confess this word through today "lord I trust you".

Journal

DECEMBER 7

Staying Power

ANCHOR SCRIPTURE: 1 CORINTHIANS 15:58 (ESV)

"Therefore, my beloved brothers, be steadfast, immovable, always abounding in the work of the Lord, knowing that in the Lord your labor is not in vain."

"Burning desire to be or do something gives us staying power - a reason to get up every morning or to pick ourselves up and start in again after a disappointment."
- *Marsha Sinetar*

PRACTICAL STEPS FOR APPLICATION:

1. Prayerfully wait on God today.

2. Appreciate God for where you are currently.

Journal

DECEMBER 8

Worry or Pray

ANCHOR SCRIPTURE: PHILIPPIANS 4:6(NLT)

"Don't worry about anything; instead, pray about everything. Tell God what you need and thank him for all he has done."

"Worry Changes Nothing, Prayer Changes Everything."

PRACTICAL STEPS FOR APPLICATION:

1. Write out those issues that troubles you and take then to the lord in prayers.

2. Meditate on the word of God often.

3. Read the book of "Matthew 6:25-34"

Journal

DECEMBER 9

Clear Vision

ANCHOR SCRIPTURE: HABAKKUK 2:2-3 (NKJV)

"Then the LORD answered me and said: "Write the vision And make it plain on tablets, That he may run who reads it. For the vision is yet for an appointed time, But at the end it shall speak, and not lie: though it tarries, wait for it; Because it will surely come, it will not tarry."

"You cannot separate good leadership from clear vision."
- *John Maxwell*

PRACTICAL STEPS FOR APPLICATION:

1. Write on paper the vision the lord has given to you.

2. Write up those vision with scriptural references.

3. Thank God always for the vision.

Journal

DECEMBER 10

The Best For Last

ANCHOR SCRIPTURE: JOHN 2:10

Everyone brings out the choice wine first and then the cheaper wine . . . but you have saved the best till now."

"Sometimes the very thing you're looking for, is the one thing you can't see."

PRACTICAL STEPS FOR APPLICATION:

1. Wait until your change comes.

2. Declare the truth of God's word concerning that present situation

Journal

DECEMBER 11

Generosity

ANCHOR SCRIPTURE: PROVERBS 11:25 (NIV)

A generous person will prosper; whoever refreshes others will be refreshed.

"Every man must decide whether he will walk in the light of creative altruism or in the darkness of destructive selfishness."
-Martin Luther King, Jr.

PRACTICAL STEPS FOR APPLICATION:

1. Give out to the less privilege

2. Speak edifying word to those that are down cast.

Journal

DECEMBER 12

Branched Off

ANCHOR SCRIPTURE: JOHN 15:5 (NIV)

"I am the vine; you are the branches. If you remain in me and I in you, you will bear much fruit; apart from me you can do nothing."

You will always be a branch, never a vine.

PRACTICAL STEPS FOR APPLICATION:

1. Stay away from every form of sin.

2. Submit to the lordship of Jesus daily by diligent obedience to his commandment.

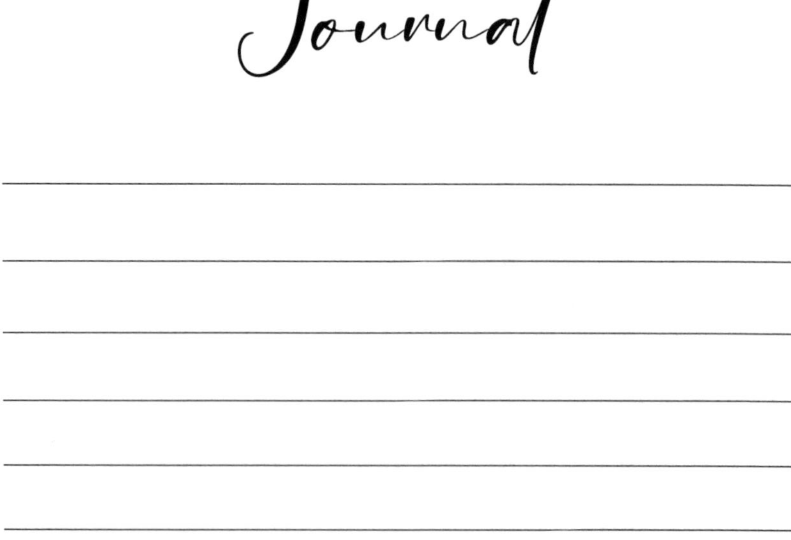

DECEMBER 13

The Great Sabotage

ANCHOR SCRIPTURE: JOHN 10:10 (NKJV)

"The thief does not come except to steal, and to kill, and to destroy. I have come that they may have life, and that they may have it more abundantly."

"I crafted most of my own tragedies without ever having even the remotest understanding that it is myself who have done the crafting."
- *Craig D. Lounsbrough*

PRACTICAL STEPS FOR APPLICATION:

1. Avoid lie and proudness.

2. Speak the truth and stay humble.

DECEMBER 14

Refreshment

ANCHOR SCRIPTURE: PSALM 23.3

He refreshes my soul.
He guides me along the right paths for his name's sake.

Love is the greatest refreshment in life.
-Pablo Picasso

PRACTICAL STEPS FOR APPLICATION:

1. Stay in God's presence by prayer and worship to him

2. Regularly attend the gathering of the believers.

Journal

DECEMBER 15

Perpetual Thanksgiving

ANCHOR SCRIPTURE: 1 THESSALONIANS 5:18

In everything give thanks: for this is the will of God in Christ Jesus concerning you.

I am grateful for what I am and have. My thanksgiving is perpetual."
- Henry David Thoreau

PRACTICAL STEPS FOR APPLICATION:

1. Thank God for health.

2. Take time to thank God for your country and your family.

Journal

DECEMBER 16

Grateful for Grace

ANCHOR SCRIPTURE: EPHESIANS 2:8 (NLT)

God saved you by his grace when you believed. And you can't take credit for this; it is a gift from God.

"In order to experience grace, we must first heal the parts of ourselves that resist it."
– Dr. Debra L. Rebel

PRACTICAL STEPS FOR APPLICATION:

1. Count all the areas of your life that grace has manifested in it and thank God for it.

2. Share with other about the grace of God upon your life.

Journal

DECEMBER 17

Cultivate Delight

ANCHOR SCRIPTURE: PSALM 37:4

Take delight in the Lord, and he will give you the desires of your heart.

True education flowers at the point when delight falls in love with responsibility.
- *Philip Pullman*

PRACTICAL STEPS FOR APPLICATION:

1. Preach the gospel to sinners.

2. Prompt obedience to the voice of God.

Journal

DECEMBER 18

Be Resilient

ANCHOR SCRIPTURE: JAMES 1:12

Blessed is the man who perseveres under trial because when he has stood the test, he will receive the crown of life that God has promised to those who love him.

"Courage doesn't always roar. Sometimes courage is the quiet voice at the end of the day saying, I will try again tomorrow."
- *Mary Anne Radmacher*

PRACTICAL STEPS FOR APPLICATION:

1. Stand on the word of God.

2. Speak rightful words.

Journal

DECEMBER 19

Called To Be Free

ANCHOR SCRIPTURE: GALATIANS 5:13

"For you were called to freedom, brethren; only do not turn your freedom into an opportunity for the flesh, but through love serve one another."

The secret to happiness is freedom...
And the secret to freedom is courage.
- Thucydides

PRACTICAL STEPS FOR APPLICATION:

1. Write out areas of your life that is held captive and declare to it "you are free"

2. Thank God for your freedom in Christ Jesus.

DECEMBER 20

Walk in Favor

ANCHOR SCRIPTURE: PSALM 5:12

"Surely, LORD, you bless the righteous; you surround them with your favor as with a shield."

"Favor is not achieved, it is received."

PRACTICAL STEPS FOR APPLICATION:

1. Boldly declare this in faith "I am highly favored".

2. Follow the leading of the holy spirit.

Journal

DECEMBER 21

A Time for Everything

ANCHOR SCRIPTURE: ECCLESIASTES 3:1

"There is a time for everything and a season for every activity under the heavens..."

The two most important requirements for major success are: first, being in the right place at the right time, and second, doing something about it.

- *Ray Kroc*

PRACTICAL STEPS FOR APPLICATION:

1. Know what the current season of your life saying.

Journal

DECEMBER 22

Way to Freedom

ANCHOR SCRIPTURE: JAMES 1:22-25

"Do not merely listen to the word, and so deceive yourselves. Do what it says. Anyone who listens to the word but does not do what it says is like a man who looks at his face in a mirror and, after looking at himself, goes away and immediately forgets what he looks like. But the man who looks intently into the perfect law that gives freedom, and continues to do this, not forgetting what he has heard, but doing it – he will be blessed in what he does."

"Between stimulus and response, there is a space.
In that space is our power to choose our response.
In our response lies our growth and our freedom."
- *Vicktor Emil Frankl*

PRACTICAL STEPS FOR APPLICATION:

1. Train your ear to hear God's voice. Be still for 15 minutes and listen.

2. Do what he asks you to do.

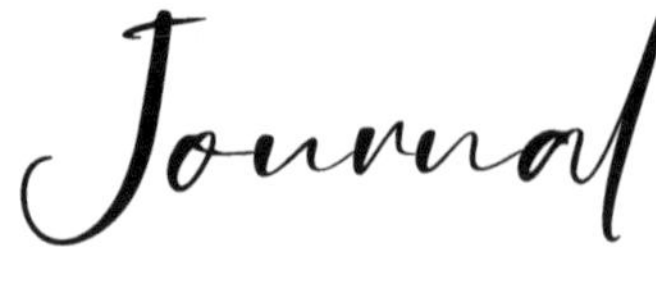

DECEMBER 23

Purpose vs. Problems

ANCHOR SCRIPTURE: PHILIPPIANS 1:21 (NIV)

"For to me, to live is Christ and to die is gain"

"The purpose of life is not to be happy. It is to be useful, to be honorable, to be compassionate, to have it make some difference that you have lived and lived well."
- *Ralph Waldo Emerson*

PRACTICAL STEPS FOR APPLICATION:

1. Wait on the lord.

2. Write those challenge that face you in trying to fulfill your purpose and ask for grace.

Journal

DECEMBER 24

Fearless

ANCHOR SCRIPTURE: 1 JOHN 4:18 (NIV)

"There is no fear in love. But perfect love drives out fear because fear has to do with punishment. The one who fears is not made perfect in love."

"Fear you have lost your hold on me"

PRACTICAL STEPS FOR APPLICATION:

1. Develop a heart of love toward God and mankind.

2. Avoid hatred and anger.

Journal

DECEMBER 25

Merry Christmas and Best Wishes for the Coming Year!

ANCHOR SCRIPTURE: PHILIPPIANS 3:13

"Brothers, I do not consider that I have made it my own. But one thing I do: forgetting what lies behind and straining forward to what lies ahead..."

"Seeking excellence means choosing to forge your own sword to cut through the limitations of your life."

-James A. Murphy

PRACTICAL STEPS FOR APPLICATION:

1. Write all the list of your achievement and thank God them.

2. Write out what you are yet to achieve and take the necessary action.

Journal

DECEMBER 26

Forge Forward

ANCHOR SCRIPTURE: 2 CORINTHIANS 9:15 (NIV)

"Thanks be to God for his indescribable gift!"

"Christmas is not a time nor a season, but a state of mind.
To cherish peace and goodwill, to be plenteous in mercy,
is to have the real spirit of Christmas."
- *Calvin Coolidge*

PRACTICAL STEPS FOR APPLICATION:

1. Write out the goals you made for this year in the journal space
2. Check the ones you have achieved already

3. Write an action plan to achieve the remaining

4. Copy this action plan and hand it over to a mentor to monitor you

DECEMBER 27

It is Not Over!

ANCHOR SCRIPTURE: EXODUS 12:1-2

"The Lord said to Moses and Aaron in Egypt, "This month is to be for you the first month, the first month of your year."

"It ain't over till it's over."
- *Yogi Berra*

PRACTICAL STEPS FOR APPLICATION:

1. Go out today and preach the gospel and lead at least a person to Christ to be born again

2. Spend tangible time giving thanks to God for the salvation of your soul.

DECEMBER 28

Changed Perspective

ANCHOR SCRIPTURE: ISAIAH 55:8 (NLT)

"My thoughts are nothing like your thoughts," says the LORD. "And my ways are far beyond anything you could imagine."

"The real voyage of discovery consists not in seeking new lands but in seeing with new eyes."
– Marcel Proust

PRACTICAL STEPS FOR APPLICATION:

1. Adequately study the word of God.

2. Stay amid people with right perspective.

Journal

DECEMBER 29

Comparison Steals Your Joy

ANCHOR SCRIPTURE: 2 CORINTHIANS 10:12 (NKJV)

"For we dare not class ourselves or compare ourselves with those who commend themselves. But they, measuring themselves by themselves, and comparing themselves among themselves, are not wise."

"Comparison is the thief of joy"
- *Theodore Roosevelt*

PRACTICAL STEPS FOR APPLICATION:

1. Avoid jealousy and know you are valued.

2. Remember, you are different on purpose and your purpose is like no other.

Journal

DECEMBER 30

Tell and Live Your Truth

ANCHOR SCRIPTURE: JOHN 8:32 (ESV)

And you will know the truth, and the truth will set you free

If you do not tell the truth about yourself,
you cannot tell it about other people.
-Virginia Woolf

PRACTICAL STEPS FOR APPLICATION:

1. Make up your mind to stop lying.

2. Determine to tell the truth.

Journal

DECEMBER 31

Faith or Feelings First

ANCHOR SCRIPTURE: JEREMIAH 17:9

The heart is deceitful above all things, and desperately sick; who can understand it?

"Feelings should follow not lead what you do"

PRACTICAL STEPS FOR APPLICATION:

1. Weigh your feeling with the truth of God's word.

2. Surrender your feeling to the Holy Spirit inside of you.

Journal

Made in the USA
Monee, IL
17 March 2022